Bud's Easy™

Research Paper Computer Manual

FOR IBM PCs

THIRD EDITION

ALVIN BARON, PH. D

LAWRENCE HOUSE PUBLISHERS
NEW YORK, NEW YORK

User's Input

Our goal is to improve this book continuously to make it easier for you to use. Here's your chance to give us your input.

Tell us:

- How you think the book can be improved.
- What you like about the book.
- What you do not like.

Send comments with your name, address, and phone number to:

Research Director
Lawrence House Publishers
500 East 77th Street
New York, New York 10162

or E-mail to:

budbooks@mindspring.com

Thanks.

First Printing, August 2000
Second Printing, March 2001 - Updated Internet Information

Trademarks

Trademarked names appear in this book. The publisher states that it used trademarked names only for editorial purposes and to the benefit of the trademark owner with no intention of infringing on those trademarks.

Every effort has been made to make this book as complete and accurate as possible, but no warranty or fitness is implied. The publisher assumes no responsibility for errors or omissions, or for damages resulting from the use of the information contained herein.

Published by Lawrence House Publishers

Contents

Part 3 Using the Publication Manual of the American Psychological Association to Write Research Papers

FOREWARD TO THE THIRD EDITION

In just a few years the Internet has become the richest source of information in the world. Not since the invention of the printing press has there been a such a powerful medium to spread knowledge to all humankind. While there are refinements to be made and problems to be solved, the Internet offers the scholarly and skilled researcher tremendous opportunities to explore vast stores of knowledge.

In this third edition we have expanded the section on Internet searching as well as the sections on writing with the computer. Illustrations have been included to make the text more easily understood. Additional Internet search sites have been added as well. We are committed to bringing our readers the very latest information on this exciting new communication tool.

HOW TO USE THIS BOOK

First, read **Chapter 1. Bud's Easy Task Method for Research Papers, Theses, and Reports** from beginning to end in order to get an overview of the planning, research methods, outlining and drafting which are necessary for writing a scholarly paper.

Second, decide, with your instructor if required, which citation style you will use to document your paper. The ***MLA Handbook*** and the ***Publication Manual of the American Psychological Association*** are the two most frequently assigned style manuals in colleges, universities and high schools. **Part 2** of this book provides details for the ***MLA Handbook*** and **Part 3** does the same for the ***Publication Manual of the APA.***

To avoid confusion, this book is color coded. All of the tabs for the *MLA Handbook* are in shades of blue, while the tabs for the ***Publication Manual of the APA* are in shades of black.** Once you decide to use one of the manuals, you need use only the part of the book you need.

Third, if you are a beginning computer user, read **Chapter 3. Basic PC Instructions** to get started with the computer. Here you will find help with turning your computer on and starting your program. You will also find instructions for basic word processing.

Fourth, locate the word processing program you will be using in either **Part 2** or **Part 3.** Tabs along the edge of the pages, color coded as noted above, will help you locate your program. Once you begin writing you will be assisted with all the mouse clicks and keystrokes you need for formatting title, bibliography, and other special pages as well as specific instructions for page numbering, setting margins, and preparing tables.

Go to it and good luck with your project!

Part One

Researching and Writing the Term Paper

Basic PC Instructions

Part One

Researching and Writing the Term Paper

Basic PC Instructions

Bud's Easy Task Method For Research Papers, Theses, And Reports

Research or term papers are assigned because writing them will enable you to:

- **learn the skills to do library research**
- **gather facts and ideas on a specific subject**
- **hone your writing skills**
- **report accurately what you have discovered**
- **provide the reader with your sources**
- **evaluate and select from among many ideas**
- **develop a thesis and defend it**
- **improve your thinking skills**

The ability to do all of these tasks will prove valuable in many future school, college, and work activities. Although writing the research paper or even the more comprehensive thesis is a challenging and demanding job, you will find that you derive much satisfaction when you submit a carefully crafted paper to you instructor.

Bud's Easy Task Method breaks the seemingly monumental assignment into a series of relatively simple tasks and provides clear instructions which make it easy to succeed. If you follow the directions you will gain confidence as you complete each task knowing that you are moving along steadily. Remember the old adage, **"The longest journey begins with a single step."** Come along now and let's take the first step toward success!

TASK 1: GET STARTED

This task is simply to get moving. Procrastination is an unhealthful way of dealing with a job you don't like. Many people delay because they are afraid of failure. You may later ease your ego pangs over a D grade by claiming, "If I'd given more time, I'd have gotten at least a B." Don't kid yourself! Be a responsible person. Get started now. Your instructor has given you directions about subjects. length, format and due dates. Be sure you understand the assignment.

Divided into a series of tasks, the writing of a term paper is not as difficult as it first appears and it can even give you lots of satisfaction. You may even enjoy it. Let's go, right now! Continue reading all of Chapter 1 to get an overview of the whole job. Then go back and complete all of the separate tasks in sequence.

TASK 2: SELECT A GENERAL TOPIC

This task is to select a general topic which will be refined to a thesis statement later. Finding a topic sometimes seems like a tough job. Your goal is to explore a meaningful subject and to offer the reader new, interesting information in a mature, scholarly manner. Controversial subjects make good topics. You should be able to describe the controversy, perhaps take sides, and find scholarly sources to support your position. However, there are many other approaches to topics. Here are some techniques to help you think of good topics for a paper.

PERSONAL INTERESTS

Make a list of your favorite subjects. Choose one and think of as many ideas about that subject as you can. For example, if you are interested in earth science, you might think of earthquakes, global warming, or floods. If you select global warming as the most interesting, ponder for a while some of the questions you have about global warming. You might want to explore the causes or effects of global warming or even discuss whether global warming is really occurring. Write the questions down to keep track of them. These questions can become good topics for your paper.

LIBRARY AND COMPUTER SOURCES

Ask your librarian for **books** on suggested research topics. Check the **tables of contents** and **indexes** of **books** on your proposed subject for ideas. Browse the **subject headings** of **newspaper** and **magazine indexes,** a **print encyclopedia** and **CD-ROM databases** if your library has them. If you can access the Internet, look at one or more **search engine directories.**

Click on a major heading, then click through all the subdirectories until you get to a list of Internet sites that interest you.

PREWRITING

The writing process requires time to reflect on and connect with your subject. The more you think about the topic before your write, the easier it will be to begin. Here are some prewriting techniques to help you connect with your topic.

Write in a Personal Journal

For your proposed topic begin listing ideas, questions, issues, quotations, summaries of newspaper articles, and notes on TV programs. You might want to include magazine article clippings and news photos, too. Write your journal without concern for punctuation and grammar. This process will help you to focus more clearly on the issues.

Free Writing

Write quickly about your topic without trying to zero in on a specific approach. Let your mind do free association and let the ideas flow. Forget grammar and style. Write without stopping. Just get your brain working. Many of the ideas from your personal journal will enter your thoughts in different ways. Don't be surprised if you generate new ideas that never occurred to you before. Review what you write. See if a topic is beginning to take shape.

Brainstorming Key Words

As you search for a topic you will come across several key words. Jot them down and brainstorm additional words or ideas that come to mind.

Main Keywords	Additional Brainstormed Words
Global Environmental Change	Emissions
	Ozone Layer
	Climate Change
	Melting Ice Caps

Clustering or Mapping

This is a technique for finding the major topics and subtopics of your subject. Start with a major word or phrase and then join other words or phrases to it with lines to show the relationships among the various words or phrases. Draw a circle around each idea. Take a close look at the map to find a possible topic or to see how your topic can be organized.

TOPIC CHECKLIST

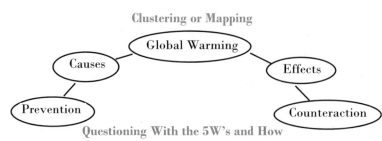

Clustering or Mapping

Questioning With the 5W's and How

Answer the questions: Who What? When? Where? Why and How? Journalists are trained to answer these questions as they write their news stories, usually highlighting the question that is the most important to the story. Use the technique as you zero in on your topic.

When you have completed all of the above, you should have a good idea for a general topic. Next you must narrow the general topic into one that is manageable, of interest to your audience, and interesting to you as well.

Study the **Topic Checklist** below. Then select your own general topic. Keep working until it passes all the Topic Checklist criteria. When you and your instructor are satisfied, go on to Task 3.

TOPIC CHECKLIST

• Not too broad	"Preparations for D-Day" **not** "Causes and Results of World War II"
• Not too narrow	"Impact of Foreign Car Imports **not** "BMW Mag Wheels"
• Interesting to readers	"Ocean Tides - Alternative Fuel" **not the obvious** "Should We Seek Other Fuels?"
• Not too technical	"Chemotherapy For Cancer" **not** Carcinoma of the Pancreas" (unless required)
• Scholarly	"Influences on Coleridge's 'Kubla Khan'"
• Interesting to you	Opens a new, challenging area to you
• OK with Instructor	Meets subject, length or other criteria

My General Topic is _____

_____

Time for Task 2: Two hours

_____

TASK 3: SEARCH FOR INFORMATION

This task is two fold: To get an overview of the subject and to determine if there is enough information of the highest quality available. Although you have selected a topic, you may find that your ideas and focus begin to change as you read.

As you read you will learn how other authors have dealt with your chosen topic. Some new issues that you had not thought of may appear. You should gradually develop your own point of view and a clearer idea of how to approach your subject. You may even change your topic!

As you begin your search, use the **Source Quality Checklist** below to help you screen potential material.

S O U R C E   Q U A L I T Y   C H E C K L I S T

Primary Sources:	First hand material such as letters, documents, novels, news stories. Excellent material.
Secondary Sources:	Material written about primary sources, events, or ideas.
• Copyright date	Most recent unless historically significant.
• Author's reputation	Well-known in field, prolific, university scholar.
• Scholarship	Material footnoted, detailed, accurate. Not from sensational, "low-brow" books or magazines.
• Relevance	Relates closely to topic.
• Objectivity	Clear point of view. Recognizes ideas of others.
• Bibliography	Extensive, scholarly sources.

BEGIN BIBLIOGRAPHY FILE COLLECTION

Today's research may involve as much non-print and electronic material as print material. As you search through card catalogs, reference books, online computer catalogs, CD-ROMs, and Internet sources, you must copy the applicable bibliographic information and locations for each book, journal or magazine article, database, or electronic source containing information on your topic.

You will need this information to compile your final bibliography and to find the books, articles, and other sources you will use for note taking.

You may use 3x5 inch cards, computer printouts, or your computer for your bibliography file. Each entry must contain as much bibliographic data as necessary for the type of reference as listed on the following pages. Assign each source a code number and write it on the upper left corner of each card, computer printout, or entry in your computer list. For each source include:

1. All the bibliographic data needed for the type of source.
2. The library call number and location to find it later.
3. Your code number.
4. Page numbers of pages with good information.
5. Your comments on the content and value of the source.
6. For Internet sources include the date you accessed the file.

A sample handwritten bibliography card is shown just below.

Sample 3x5 Inch Bibliography Card

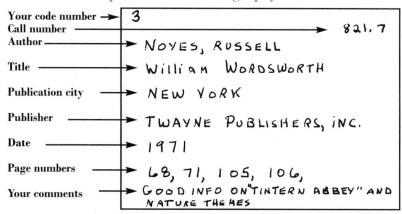

Your code number → 3

Call number → 821.7

Author → NOYES, RUSSELL

Title → William WORDSWORTH

Publication city → NEW YORK

Publisher → TWAYNE PUBLISHERS, INC.

Date → 1971

Page numbers → 68, 71, 105, 106,

Your comments → GOOD INFO ON "TINTERN ABBEY" AND NATURE THEMES

COMPUTER BIBLIOGRAPHY FILE

You can also maintain your file of bibliography "cards" on your computer. Open a file named, **Bibliography.** If you are using a laptop in the library, you can type bibliographic data directly. If your computer is at home, prepare a handwritten bibliography card and enter the data from the card to your file later. Type an underline after each entry to separate them. The computer file will not be alphabetical, so be prepared to print and cut the entries into strips to alphabetize them for the final bibliography list later.

Sample Entry in Your Computer Bibliography File

Bibliography Document →

Code Number →

Bibliographic Data →

Call Number →

Location →

Good Pages →

Your Comments →

Bibliography.doc - Microsoft Word

File Edit View Insert Format Tools Table Window Help

100% · Hyperlink · Times New Roman · **B** *I* U

Code # 3

Noyes, Russell. <u>William Wordworth</u>. News York: Twayne publishers, Inc., 1971

Call # 821.7

Located in stacks – Main Reading Room

See Pages 68, 71, 105, 106

Comment: Good info on "Tintern Abbey" and nature themes

Page 3   Sec 1   3/3   At 1.6"   Ln 3   Col 11

Start   B   9:58 PM

BIBLIOGRAPHIC INFORMATION REQUIRED FOR VARIOUS SOURCES

BOOKS

Author's name
Title of the book part (an introduction, essay or poem, etc.)
Title of the book
Name of editor or translator
Edition
Number(s) of volume(s)
Series name
Publication city
Publisher
Publication date
Page number(s)

PERIODICALS - MAGAZINES AND JOURNALS

Author's name
Title of article
Periodical name
Series number
Volume number
Issue number
Publication date
Page number(s)

CD-ROMS BASED ON A PRINTED DATABASE

Author's name
Publication information for the printed database.
Database title underlined
Publication medium (CD-ROM)
Vendor's name if relevant
Electronic publication date

CD-ROMS NOT BASED ON A PRINTED DATABASE

Author's name
Title of material in quotation marks
Date of material
Database title underlined
Publication medium (CD-ROM)
Vendor's name if relevant
Electronic publication date

DISKETTE OR MAGNETIC TAPE

Author's name
Title of part of work in quotation marks
Title of product underlined
Edition, release, or version
Publication medium (Diskette or Magnetic tape)
Publication city
Publisher
Publication date

MATERIAL FROM COMPUTER SERVICES BASED ON A PRINTED SOURCE

Author's name
Publication information for the printed source
Title of database underlined
Publication medium (Online)
Computer service name
Access date

MATERIAL FROM COMPUTER SERVICE NOT BASED ON A PRINTED SOURCE

Author's name
Title of material in quotation marks
Date
Title of database underlined
Publication medium (Online)
Computer service name
Access date

ELECTRONIC JOURNALS, NEWSLETTERS, AND CONFERENCES
Author's name
Title of article or document in quotation marks
Title of journal, newsletter, or, conference underlined
Volume or issue number
Publication date in parenthesis
Number of pages if given or *n. page.*
Publication medium (Online)
Computer network name
Access date

ELECTRONIC TEXTS
Author's name
Text title underlined
Publication information for printed source
Publication medium (Online)
Repository of the electronic text
Computer network name
Access date

TELEVISION OR RADIO PROGRAMS
Title of episode in quotation marks
Program title underlined
Names of pertinent performers, writers, directors, producers.
Series title if any
Network name
Station call letters and city
Broadcast date

CONDUCTING RESEARCH IN THE LIBRARY

Libraries have changed dramatically and will continue to change as a result of the electronic and computer revolution. Research has become easier and faster since we can use computers to find sources. We can search many reference tools without having to schlep piles of books from dusty stacks only to discover that most are useless to us. Most important, more and more data is being recorded electronically so the amount of material available on all subjects is increasing dramatically.

Today we are beginning to speak of the "virtual library" because we can go beyond the walls of the traditional library to access data in distant libraries, in commercial databases, and in other computers around the world from our computer terminals. Nevertheless, many of the tools of research remain the same whether we access them in print or electronically.

EXPLORING YOUR LIBRARY

Begin by visiting your library and reading any student handbooks available or attending an orientation lecture. You will save time and avoid missteps if you are familiar with your library's facilities and the location of various departments.

If your library has not yet computerized, you will deal with card catalogs and a reference section. The search should be straightforward. You will be using 3 x 5 cards for your bibliography file. Be sure to ask the librarian(s) for help. They love to be of assistance and are specially trained in research techniques.

On the other hand, if you are at a college or university or a more modern high school or public library, you will have to become acquainted with the electronic tools available. You can access separate library collections and even reach into the catalogs and resources of other libraries. You may be able to do research and possibly even access library resources from your computer at home, in your dorm, or computer center.

A good place to begin after your initial orientation is at a computer screen. If you are in the library, hitting the ESC or Enter key will usually bring up the **library's home page.** If away and your library is on the Internet, log on and type the URL (Internet address) of your library and its home page will appear. If your are unfamiliar with the Internet, see **pages 1-27 to 1-30** for help. Typically, you will see "links" to one or more of the following: **a student handbook, instructions for the online catalog, descriptions of special collections such as reference and multimedia, connections to other libraries within and outside your school, and possibly Internet services.** Clicking on any of the underlined links will bring up the corresponding page.

SEARCH TOOLS

Libraries are filled with special search tools. Be sure to use as many as possible to help you in your search for information.

Powerful tools for library research include:

◆ **General Catalogs - Online and Card**
◆ **Reference Section**

■ **Encyclopedias**	■ **Dictionaries**
■ **Biographies**	■ **Bibliographies**
■ **Yearbooks**	■ **Abstracts**
■ **Research Guides**	■ **Statistical Information**
■ **Indexes**	■ **Multimedia Collections**

SEARCH 1: SEARCH THE ONLINE CATALOG

Systems vary so you will have to learn your library's procedures by following the instructions on the terminal, attending orientation lectures, or reading instructional pamphlets. Most screens have easy to follow directions. The first screen may offer options such as restricting the search to holdings at one library building or extending the search to other libraries. Some systems allow you to search within a range of publication years or by type of source such as films or electronic journals. You can choose these options by clicking on the appropriate boxes on the screen.

Typical Online Catalog - First Screen

Library online catalogs will vary, but the illustrations below are typical. The catalog in this illustration offers indexes beginning with **General Keyword.** Begin your search by selecting the index you want to search. In the example below, the student selected General Keyword from among the choices in the list. This system outlines the index selected in blue. Under the index list the screen describes what the selected index contains. In this case, it is **"General Search of Major Fields."**

Typical First Screen of Online Catalog

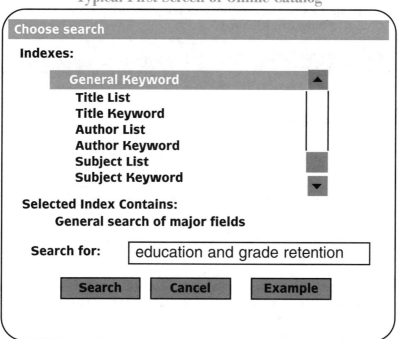

Choose search

Indexes:

> **General Keyword**
> **Title List**
> **Title Keyword**
> **Author List**
> **Author Keyword**
> **Subject List**
> **Subject Keyword**

Selected Index Contains:
General search of major fields

Search for: education and grade retention

[**Search**] [**Cancel**] [**Example**]

Most systems allow you to refine searches with **Boolean logic** (see **Internet Search pages 1-33 to 1-34 for details**) which uses the words, **and, not,** and **or.** For example, this student was researching the topic, "**social promotion,**" the practice of promoting failing students to the next grade. She entered "**education and grade retention**" as keywords in the **Search for: box.** The student then clicked on the **Search Button** at the bottom of the screen. The computer searched its database to find all the books in the collection which have information on both keywords. As you can see, the screen also offers options to cancel the search and to view an example of a source. **See the Typical First Screen of Online Catalog on page 1-11.**

Typical Second Screen of Online Catalog

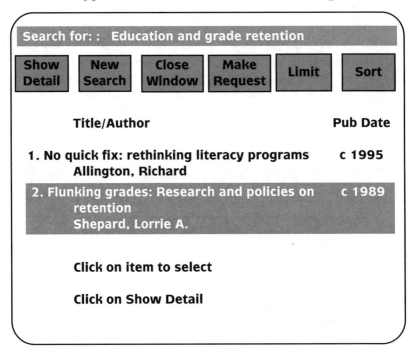

> **Search for: :   Education and grade retention**
>
> | **Show Detail** | **New Search** | **Close Window** | **Make Request** | **Limit** | **Sort** |
> |---|---|---|---|---|---|
>
> **Title/Author**   **Pub Date**
>
> **1. No quick fix: rethinking literacy programs   c 1995**
>   **Allington, Richard**
>
> **2. Flunking grades: Research and policies on   c 1989**
>   **retention**
>   **Shepard, Lorrie A.**
>
> **Click on item to select**
>
> **Click on Show Detail**

This online catalog yielded two titles, No Quick Fix and Flunking Grades. See the illustration, **Typical Second Screen of Online Catalog** just above.

The student noted the instruction on the bottom of the screen: **Click on item to select.** She clicked on the book that looked very good, *Flunking grades: research and policies on retention.* **She also** clicked on **Show Detail** to get more information.

The third screen appeared with the following information about the book:

> **Call number**
> **Status showing that the book has been checked in**
> **Full title**
> **Publisher**
> **Description showing volume, number of pages, illustrations, and book size.**
> **A note that the book is part of a series.**
> **A note that the book contains a bibliography and index**
> **A note showing other related subjects.**

Typical Third Screen of Online Catalog

Bibliographic Detail: Title 1 of 2

Call Number: LB3063.f57 1989   **Status:** Checked in

Title: Flunking grades: Research and policies on retention/edited by Lorrie A. Shepard and Mary Lee Smith

Publisher: London; New York: Falmer Press, 1989

Description: viii, 243 p.: ill; 24 cm

Series: Education policy perspectives

Bibliography: Includes bibliography and index

Subjects: Promotion (School-United States)

The information about the series and other subjects is underlined, which indicates that these are "links." Clicking on the underlined words will open more pages with further information. See the illustration, **Typical Third Screen of Online Catalog** just above.

Your library catalog may be different. Take some time to learn it. Ask your librarian for help. Get the sources and skim the tables of contents and indexes of the books to find information. Use the **Source Quality Checklist** on **page 1-5.** Try to locate at least five good sources.

As indicated above, you must be sure to prepare a "bibliography entry" for each source. In addition to 3 x 5 inch cards and your own computer file, if your library online catalog is able, you can print out the screens with bibliographic details. Obtaining a printout will save you much copying and avoid errors in transcribing.

Write the page number on which you find relevant material on the bibliography printouts and jot comments describing the material. Remember to assign your personal source code on each bibliography entry. The illustration below shows how the student wrote on the printout of the last screen and used it as a bibliography "card."

Library Catalog Printout Used as Bibliography Entry

Code 6

Pages:
171-172

Bibliographic Detail: Title 1 of 2

Call Number: LB3063.f57 1989   Status: Checked in

Title: Flunking grades: Research and policies on →
→ retention/edited by Lorrie A. Shepard and →
→ Mary Lee Smith¶
¶
Publisher: London; New York: Falmer Press, 1989¶
¶
Description: viii, 243 p.: ill; 24 cm¶
¶
Series: Education policy perspectives¶
¶
Bibliography: Includes bibliography and index¶
¶
Subjects: Promotion (School-United States)

Comment

Excellent statistics on drop-out rates for those left back compared with rates for those moved ahead.

Be sure you have all the information required for the source as shown on **pages 1-7 to 1-9.**

If abstracts or full text printouts are available, skim to see if the information is of value. Get the valuable abstracts or full text printouts and put them aside for **Task 7. Classify Note Sources To Match Sentence Outline.**

UNDERSTANDING LIBRARY CLASSIFICATION SYSTEMS

Libraries use either the Dewey Decimal Classification System or the Library of Congress Classification System. Become familiar with the systems and you will feel more comfortable with your searches.

DEWEY DECIMAL CLASSIFICATION

The chart below illustrates the main classes and subdivisions of the Dewey Decimal Classification system.

000   **Generalities**

100   **Philosophy and Psychology**

200   **Religion**

300   **Social Sciences**

400   **Language**

500   **Natural Sciences and Mathematics**

600   **Technology (Applied Sciences)**

700   **The Arts**

800   **Literature and Rhetoric**

900   **Geography and History**

DEWEY DECIMAL SYSTEM

The Dewey Decimal Classification is used by most public libraries and school libraries. The system is divided into ten main classes. Each main class is further divided into ten divisions, and each division into ten sections. The first digit in each three-digit number represents the main class. For example, 500 represents natural sciences and mathematics and is used for general works in the science.

The second digit in each three digit number indicates the division. For example, 510 is used for mathematics, 520 for astronomy, and 530 for physics. The third digit in each three digit number indicates the section. Thus, 530 is used for general works on physics, 531 for classical mechanics, 532 for fluid mechanics.

A decimal point follows the third digit in a class number after which division by ten continues to the specific degree of classification needed. Following or directly beneath the classification numerals, you may also find additional numerals and/or letters which are derived from the "Cutter Table" used for further information about the book or author.

For example, the title, *Freedom From Fear: the American People in Depression and War, 1929-1945* by David Kennedy, is classified as 973.91 K indicating all the divisions and sub-divisions under the 970 heading, General History of North America. The letter K designates the first letter of the author's last name.

LIBRARY OF CONGRESS CLASSIFICATION SYSTEM

The chart below illustrates the main divisions of the Library of Congress Classification System.

A General Works

B Philosophy, Psychology, Religion

C History - Auxiliary Sciences

D History - American

E & F History: American

F Geography, Anthropology

H Social Sciences

J Political Science

K Law

L Education

M Music

N Fine Arts

P Language and Literature

Q Science

R Medicine

S Agriculture

T Technology

U Military Science

V Naval Science

Z Bibliography and Library Science

I,O,W,X, and Y are not being used. They are available for future expansion and for classifying knowledge yet to be discovered.

The Library of Congress system uses a series of letters rather than numerals for the major divisions. All numbers can begin with one, two, or three letters. The first letter of a call number represents one of the 21 major divisions of the LC system. For most of the subject areas, the single letter represents books of a general nature for that subject area. Examples are Q - General Science or E - History - American.

The title, *Freedom From Fear: The American People in Depression and War, 1929-1945* by David Kennedy, has the call number E173.094 vol. 9

The call number contains all the letters and numerals that identify the divisions and sub-divisions of the Library of Congress system. The first set of numbers in a call number helps to define a book's subject. The numbers 173 in the example tells us that the book deals with Sources and Documents while the .094 offers further classification

The Library of Congress also uses the Cutter system for refining classifications related to the author and other works by the same author.

SEARCH 2: SEARCH THE CARD CATALOG

Some libraries have not yet switched entirely to online catalogs while others still retain all or part of their collections in card catalogs. Ask the librarian to ascertain the status of your library's cataloging. If a card catalog exists, you will have to search it.

Look through the subject and author-title catalog drawers. Try to locate at least five sources on your topic. Complete a 3 x 5 inch bibliography card or make an entry in your computer Bibliography file for each book. Locate the books in the stacks or other location. Skim the tables of contents and indexes to find information on your topic. Write the page numbers on which you find good material and jot a comment describing the information. Remember to assign each book a code number. See the **Sample Bibliography Card on page 1-4.**

SEARCH 3: SEARCH THE REFERENCE SECTION

For an overview of your subject begin with standard reference works. Every field has specialized reference books such as encyclopedias, indexes, bibliographies, research guides, biographical indexes, and statistical summaries. Librarians love to help with research so don't be shy about asking for assistance. They can steer you to the best reference sources.

Reference works will be found in **print**, in **CD-ROMs**, in **online data bases** or in **microform.** Print material is generally arranged by subject with encyclopedias and dictionaries about the same subject shelved together. Annual publications like bibliographies and indexes like the *Reader's Guide to Periodical Literature* are usually shelved in one place.

CD-ROMs containing the contents of encyclopedias, indexes, and other databases may be inserted into your personal computer or may be installed in the library's online system. Databases from other libraries or commercial vendors can also be retrieved, but some suppliers charge fees for this service. Remember that you may be able to access CD-ROMs and databases from your own PC through the Internet. More on this later in the chapter.

CD-ROMs and online databases have the advantages of being more current and more inclusive than corresponding print material. In addition, your library may enable you to download data directly to a disk which you can later load directly to your PC. Some libraries even sell blank disks for a minimal charge if you forget your own.

SEARCH 3. 1: SEARCH ENCYCLOPEDIAS

General encyclopedias are OK for preliminary research to give you an overview of your topic. They provide good overall coverage of most important persons, events, and topics, but you must go beyond them. Some encyclopedias are available in CD-ROM format or online. They may or may not be in your library database.

GENERAL ENCYCLOPEDIAS
Encyclopedia Americana
New Encyclopedia Britannica

Special encyclopedias for most specific disciplines are published. Check with your librarian for the encyclopedia(s) in your field.

TYPICAL SPECIAL ENCYCLOPEDIAS
Encyclopedia of Asian History
Encyclopedia of the Biological Sciences
Encyclopedia of Psychology
Encyclopedia of Social Work
Encyclopedia of World Art

SEARCH 3. 2: SEARCH INDEXES

Indexes contain alphabetically arranged information from magazines, scholarly journals, newspapers, and other sources. They are published periodically and are usually bound in volumes containing a range of dates. General indexes catalog articles from popular newspapers and magazines. Specialized indexes catalog articles from journals within a discrete discipline. Many indexes are now on CD-ROM and are included in most library databases. If so, both the general and special subject indexes will be available, frequently with abstracts and full text printouts. Ask your librarian for help in finding the print special indexes.

POPULAR GENERAL INDEXES
Expanded Academic ASAP
Infotrac
National Newspaper Index
New York Times Index
Reader's Guide to Periodical Literature
Wilson Select

TYPICAL SPECIAL INDEXES
Art Index
Education Index
General Science Index
Literary Criticism Index
Medline

SEARCH 3. 3: SEARCH BIBLIOGRAPHIES

Bibliographies contain lists of publications. There are bibliographies of bibliographies, bibliographies of general subjects, and bibliographies of special fields. There are even bibliographies of reference books - a good place to start.

As with other reference works, some are available on CD-ROM and in online databases and some are not. The general bibliographies listed on the next page will lead you to lists of books which contain bibliographies of your subject.

POPULAR GENERAL BIBLIOGRAPHIES
Bibliographic Index: A Cumulative Bibliography of Bibliographies
The New York Times Guide To Reference Materials
Subject Guide to Books In Print

TYPICAL SPECIAL BIBLIOGRAPHIES
American Women and Politics
Bibliographic Guide to Black Studies
Bibliographic Guide to Business and Economics
MLA Bibliography
Political Science: A Bibliographic Guide to the Literature

SEARCH 3. 4: SEARCH ABSTRACTS

Almost every discipline publishes volumes which summarize articles from the journals in the field. If you find an abstract which looks valuable, get the journal and read the full text. If the journal is not in the library, it is permissible to cite information from an abstract as long as you use the appropriate citation. Many abstracts are now on CD-ROM and in online databases with full text available. Ask your librarian for the abstracts which are published in your field and check the online database in the library.

TYPICAL SPECIAL SUBJECT ABSTRACTS
Art Abstracts
Biological Abstracts
Education Abstracts
Historical Abstracts
Newspaper Abstracts
Periodical Abstracts
Psychological Abstracts
Sociological Abstracts

SEARCH 3. 5: SEARCH RESEARCH GUIDES

Research guides usually contain reference tools and other sources available for research in a particular discipline. Ask your librarian for the latest research guides in your area of research. Check to see if any are available on CD-ROM or in online databases. See a list of typical research guides on the next page.

TYPICAL RESEARCH GUIDES
Information Sources in Economics
Library Research Guide to History
Literary Research Guide

SEARCH 3. 6: SEARCH DICTIONARIES

Dictionaries contain alphabetically arranged brief definitions within specific disciplines. Excellent for obtaining precise meanings of unfamiliar terms in your area of research. Check with your librarian for a dictionary in your subject. Check your library's online database for electronic dictionaries.

TYPICAL DICTIONARIES
American Dictionary of Economics
Black's Law Dictionary
Dictionary of Biology
Dictionary of Botany
Dictionary of Music
Dictionary of Philosophy
Dictionary of the Social Sciences

SEARCH 3. 7: SEARCH BIOGRAPHICAL SOURCES

Volumes of biographical data are published for persons living and dead. In addition, some disciplines publish biographical data on prominent persons in specific fields. If your research deals with a person, these sources will provide brief biographical summaries which can serve as a starting point before going on to full biographies. Some biographical sources are available in electronic format.

POPULAR BIOGRAPHICAL SOURCES FOR LIVING PERSONS
Biography Index
Current Biography
Who's Who in America
International Who's Who

POPULAR BIOGRAPHICAL SOURCES FOR DEAD PERSONS
American National Biography
Webster's New Biographical Dictionary

TYPICAL BIOGRAPHICAL SOURCES IN SPECIFIC DISCIPLINES
Who's Who in Religion
American Men and Women of Science
Biographical Dictionary of Women Artists in Europe and America Since 1850
Dictionary of American Negro Biography
Dictionary of Literary Biography
Who's Who in Religion

SEARCH 3. 8: SEARCH YEARBOOKS

Yearbooks contain information about specific personalities, discoveries, inventions, or other events which occurred during a specific year. To locate such current information use one of the following.

TYPICAL YEARBOOKS
Americana Annual
Britannica Book of the Year

SEARCH 3. 9: SEARCH STATISTICAL SOURCES

Statistical data is available from many sources, particularly government agencies. If your research deals with such data, ask your librarian for help finding specialized statistical information. Much statistical information is available in electronic format.

STATISTICAL DATA PUBLICATIONS
Demographic Yearbook
Statistical Abstract of the United States
Statistical Yearbook

SEARCHING WITH CD-ROMs OR ONLINE DATABASES

This search may be your most productive, so you will have to learn the way to access your library's CD-ROM collections and its databases since systems vary. To search CD-ROMs or online databases follow the instructions in your library's handbook, on the terminal, or ask a librarian for help.

A nice feature of electronic encyclopedias is the incorporation of graphics and sound so you can actually hear famous speeches and see color photos of things. Some electronic dictionaries provide correct spoken pronunciation of words.

CD-ROM or online indexes hold much more information and are quicker and easier to use than print indexes. Many indexes contain abstracts and full-texts of articles, so you can quickly tell whether the article will be of use in your research. Remember, too, that every library cannot afford to purchase every index or every journal in each index so don't be surprised if you cannot retrieve some sources.

Follow the instructions on the terminal. The first screen will usually provide a list of databases by subject These may include abstracts, indexes, bibliographies, and other reference tools. The collection within each database will vary from library to library.

The illustration below shows a typical first screen of an online database collection.

Typical First Screen of Online Databases
Showing Databases by Subject

Databases by Title
Databases by Vendor

Databases by Subject

Databases by Subject
Table of Contents
Art & Humanities
Biography
Biology & Marine Science
Business
Education
General
General Science
Government
Law
Library Science
Literature
Medical
Music
News
Political Science
Psychology
Social Sciences

● Available only from library workstations
⊥⊥ Indicates full-text available

(Click on underlined links to access databases)
GENERAL

- Article1st ● ⊥⊥
- Contents1st ●
- Expanded Academic ASAP ⊥⊥
- FactSearch ●
- FastDoc ● ⊥⊥
- FirstSearch ● ⊥⊥
- GPO (Government Printing Office)
- GPO (for Windows 95 and higher)
- Infotrac ⊥⊥
- A Matter of Fact
- A Matter of Fact (for Windows 95 and higher)
- NetFirst ●
- PA Research II Periodicals ⊥⊥
- Periodical Abstracts ● ⊥⊥
- Periodical Contents Index ●
- Readers' Guide Abstracts ● ⊥⊥
- Wilson Select ● ⊥⊥

On the left is a list of databases by subject. In this illustration, a student writing a paper on the **Kosovo war** was interested in **President Clinton's role.** She clicked on the **General link** in the **Databases by Subject** list on the left side of the screen.

From the list of databases under the **General** heading the student decided to search the **Readers' Guide Abstracts.** This is a database which contains abstracts of articles which appear in the magazines and newspapers which the **Readers' Guide** indexes. She clicked on the **Readers' Guide Abstracts link**. The second page opened which described the type of periodicals, dates of publication, update periods, and availability of full texts in the database.

At the top of the screen is a **search box.** Our student typed **"Kosovo and Clinton"** in the **Search for** box and clicked on the **Start Search** button. See the illustration of the second screen just below.

Typical Second Screen of Online Databases Showing Selected Database

Welcome to *Readers' Guide Abstracts !* By doing a search, you agree to the OCLC Terms and the Readers' Guide Abstracts Terms and Conditions.

Word, Phrase (Help)   Keyword Index (Help)

Search for Kosovo and Clinton   **in** Abstract   Browse Index

Start Search   History...   Advanced Search

FirstSearch Database

H.W. Wilson   **Readers' Guide Abstracts**

Description	Popular periodicals published in the U.S. and Canada. Includes current events and news, fine arts, fashion, education, business, sports, health and nutrition, consumer affairs, and others.
Records	1100 K
Dates Covered	1983-01-01 ... (Indexing); 1984-03-01 ... (Abstracting)
Updated	Monthly
Full Text	Yes (Check with your librarian for availability)

The third screen opened showing the search results. See the illustration below showing the third screen. At the top of the screen you can see the results of the search which found 161 records. The page will usually show the first ten sources (only six are shown in this illustration) which contain the keywords entered in the Search box.

Our researcher clicked on **Number 2. NATO's battle within: is leadership missing?** to open the next screen with an abstract of the article and full bibliographic data. **See the illustration of the fourth screen on page 1- 26.**

A note at the top indicates that this library owns the item. Clicking on the **Get/Display Item** will open the full text of the article. In most libraries you will be able to print out the abstract page or the full text pages and/or download to your own disk. The **Libraries with Item** button will yield a list of local libraries which have the article. The **E-Mail Record** button will open a screen that asks you to which e-mail address you want the item sent!

**Typical Third Screen of Online Databases
Showing Initial Search Results**

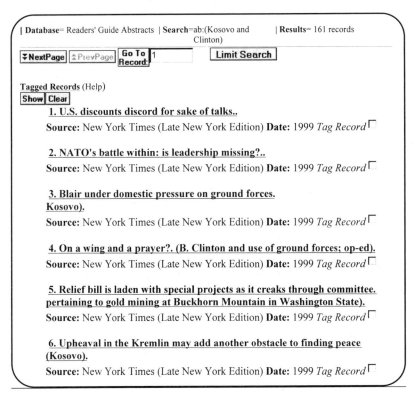

SEARCH ONLINE DATABASES

You can use the abstract printout as your bibliography card since all the bibliographic information is there and you eliminate any chances of error in copying. Be sure to add your code number in one corner of the printout. You may want to add handwritten notes or underline or highlight text.

Typical Fourth Screen of Online Databases
Showing The Abstract of the Selected Source

[**Database**= Readers' Guide Abstracts | **Search**=ab:(Kosovo and Clinton) | **Results**= 161 records | **Record**=2]

Libraries with Item Get / Display Item E-Mail Record

⇟ NextRec ⇞ PrevRec

Ownership: FirstSearch indicates your library owns this item or magazine.

```
    NUMBER: BRGA99032713
    AUTHOR: Gordon, Michael R.
     TITLE: NATO's battle within: is leadership missing?.
    SOURCE: New York Times (Late New York Edition) (May 20 '99) p. A14
STANDARD NO: 0362-4331
      DATE: 1999
RECORD TYPE: art
  CONTENTS: feature article
  ABSTRACT: President Clinton continues to wrestle over the question of
            whether to dispatch combat forces to Kosovo, and without clear
            direction from Washington, NATO's strategy for bringing the
            war to a successful close has begun to unravel.  The British,
            Germans, and Italians are all on separate pages with regard to
            the issue of ground troops in Kosovo, and this confusion
            within NATO is undoubtedly welcome news for President Slobodan
            Milosevic of Yugoslavia, whose strategy from the start has
            been to survive the air war, encourage divisions within the
            Western alliance, and attempt to negotiate a Kosovo settlement
            on his terms.
   SUBJECT: Kosovo (Serbia)  - History - Civil War, 1998-  - American
            participation.Kosovo (Serbia)  - History - Civil War, 1998-  -
            Ground troops.Kosovo (Serbia)  - History - Civil War, 1998-  -
            NATO participation.
```

⇟ NextRec ⇞ PrevRec

SEARCHING MICROFORM SOURCES

Microforms are print materials which have been photographically reduced to very small size on film to save much needed space. These films are known as **microcard, microfilm**, and **microfiche** (*microfeesh*) depending on the technology used. The library maintains special machines called "readers" which enlarge the print and enable you to read the material.

Typically, libraries use microform for old copies of newspapers, magazines, or journals which because of age would dry up and fall apart if left in their original states. If you are doing historical research and need information that is very old, you will probably find it in the library's microform collection. Ask your librarian for help.

CONCLUDING LIBRARY RESEARCH

When you have searched all the library's resources for information on your topic, you should have a large stack of bibliography cards and/or printouts or you should have a fairly lengthy list of bibliographic entries in your computer "Bibliography File." Be sure each entry has your code number, the library's call number, the location in the library, and, most important, your notes about the information you found on your topic. You should be thoroughly immersed in the subject and have a good idea of how other writers have dealt with the topic.

The next step is to search the Internet if you or your library has a modem, a high speed DSL line, a T1 line or other connection.

WHAT IS THE INTERNET?

The Internet is a network of millions (and the number is increasing daily) of interconnected computers worldwide. No one owns the Internet and it has no central facility. Nevertheless, this remarkable electronic communication network enables users to:

- **Send and receive electronic mail**
- **Join special interest groups**
- **Discuss common topics in real time**
- **Search for information on a wide range of subjects**
- **Download text, graphics, sound, and software.**

HOW THE INTERNET WORKS - INTERNET PROTOCOLS

Communication is established between computers through special systems called **protocols.** Usually the name of the protocol forms part of the address. The most frequently used protocols are:

E-mail: Send and receive messages worldwide, usually in seconds, to individual mailbox addresses. Photos, text and other files may be attached.

Listserv: Participate in e-mail discussions on specific subjects, frequently academic, conducted by organizations. You must subscribe by sending an e-mail to a *listserver* which transmits messages to and from subscribers.

Usenet News: Participate in discussions in newsgroups. Messages about many topics are exchanged among *newsgroups* on electronic bulletin boards. *Newsgroups* are different from *listservs* in that messages are stored on computers and users must log on to read messages. Some newsgroups are academic but topics vary widely. Newsgroups are definitely not recommended as sources for serious research because it is difficult to assess the quality of information or the authority of the writer.

FTP: **File Transfer Protocol** is used to transfer computer files including pictures, sounds, software, and text to your computer. Many sites are restricted to those who have an account which allows users to access and download information. However, most public agencies allow free access to anyone using the username, ***anonymous***, to log on and download files.

Gopher: With the rapid growth and technological development of the World Wide Web, gopher sites have gradually begun to disappear, but they can be accessed on the Internet. Gopher is more like a regular library subject catalog and it will search the holdings of many computers for your subject.

Telnet: Telnet is a protocol which enables you to log on to another computer and use it as your own. Connections in some schools and universities allow students to use large computers from their homes or dorms.

THE WORLD WIDE WEB

As the Internet grew, scientists developed an umbrella shell called the **World Wide Web** which provides easier access to the Internet protocols described above. The Web uses an interface based on **hypertext** which is a technique of linking words or pictures to other files. Information is retrieved on the Web through **hypertext documents** which are capable of holding text, graphics, and sound. Hypertext documents use a special language called **HyperText Markup Language** or **html.** To access a hypertext document on the Web you must use the letters **http** for *HyperText Transfer Protocol.*

The first hypertext document you see when you reach a site is called a **"home page."** Each page contains **underlined** and **highlighted words** or **graphics** which are links to other Internet sites. By clicking on the links, the user opens the next page which can contain images, video, sound, and text. The whole is a "web" of links which can produce an amazing array of information.

URL: UNIFORM RESOURCE LOCATOR OR INTERNET ADDRESS

The **URL** is the address of sites on the Internet. Internet addresses are similar to regular mail addresses, but look more complicated. The **protocol name** always begins a URL whether it is an **http, gopher,** or **FTP** site. The URL contains a series of network names separated by dots (**.**), slashes (**/**), and tildes (**~**).

URLs are very specific. Some are case sensitive, which means if some of the letters are capitalized, the user must be sure those are capitalized when typing the address. An extra space, period, or other miscue will make it impossible to reach the site.

INTERNET ADDRESS DOMAINS:

.com....**commercial and business**	.aero.........**air industry**
.edu.....**educational institutions**	.biz............**general use**
.gov.....**government agencies**	.coop.........**business cooperatives**
.mil.....**military organizations**	.info...........**general use**
.net.....**network resources**	.museum....**museums**
.org.....**other organizations**	.name........**personal web sites**
.pro.....**professionals such as doctors and lawyers**	

For example, *http://starburst.uscolo.edu* means there is a sub-network called **starburst** connected to a network at the **University of Southern Colorado** and it is an **educational institution**. A two letter country abbreviation usually ends the address when a country is designated. The address, *http://www.ed.gov*, is the **U.S. Department of Education Online Library**. **E-mail** user's names are placed at the beginning and followed with the @ sign. Thus, *kwilliams@delaware.udel.edu* is the address of **K. Williams** at the **University of Delaware**.

IMPORTANT: **Internet addresses, URLs, frequently change, move, or disappear. Don't be surprised if you cannot access a URL. If stymied, your best bet is to use the major part of the URL at the left of the address followed by the domain. The home page should open with links to the site you are trying to reach.**

INTERNET SERVICE PROVIDERS

Internet service providers are the organizations, usually commercial, that hook you up to the Internet. Popular ISPs are **AOL, Mindspring,** and **Earthlink,** but there are many more. Most charge a monthly fee or a fee based on usage.

Connections are provided in several ways. **Modems** connect through an existing phone line. Service is slow and the phone line cannot be used while connected. **Digital Subscriber Lines (DSL)** are connected through phone lines, are much faster, allow simultaneous use of the phone line, and are always "on" so there is no need to dial up the connection. **TV cable companies** provide services similar to DSL. **T1** lines are the fastest but most expensive. With the proliferation of handheld devices, wireless connections are now available and are becoming more common.

Once you are connected, the ISP's home page appears. The page will resemble a typical **windows application window** complete with a **Menu Bar and Tool Bar.** Most home pages can be modified to suit the individual user.

WEB BROWSERS

Several "browsers" or programs for accessing the Internet are available such as **Netscape Navigator, Microsoft Explorer, and Mosaic.** The browser is the device which lets you access the Internet. Learn the uses of your browser's **File, Edit, Favorites** or **Bookmark, Back, Forward, Help** and other buttons on the **Button Bar.**

CONDUCTING RESEARCH ON THE INTERNET

Information consisting of articles, graphics, video, sound, and software resides in the millions of computers which make up the Internet. This information can be obtained with amazing speed as compared with research in a conventional library. However, the Internet is like a vast library which has no regular system of cataloging such as the Dewey Decimal System or the Library of Congress Catalog. Therefore, finding the material you need requires some special knowledge of the Internet.

The good news is that advances in search techniques are rapidly making searching simpler, faster, and more precise. The following pages will empower you to get the most out of this vast, rich, and valuable information resource.

SEARCH TOOLS

Conducting a thorough search will require you to use all of the search tools available on the Internet. You should use each systematically to insure that you have made an exhaustive search for all the significant material on your topic.

Powerful tools for searching are available including:

◆ **Search Engines**
◆ **Invisible Web Search Engines**
◆ **Meta-Search Engines**
◆ **Subject Directories**
◆ **Periodical Guides**
◆ **Book Guides**
◆ **Guides to Other Library Collections and Resources**
◆ **Listserv Mailing Lists Guides**
◆ **E-mail Address Guides**
◆ **Usenet Newsgroups Guides**

SEARCH 1: SEARCH WITH A SEARCH ENGINE

Read the entire section on search engines to learn about them before you begin to use this tool. Search engines can access most of the Internet protocols including gopher and FTP, but each differs in the manner of searching and in the files which it searches. All search engines will present a list of sites based on the **key words** you use in the query. The list will include hypertext links which are underlined and highlighted. Clicking on a links will bring a new page to your computer screen.

Each search engine's home page layout will be different. Search engines are continually improving and adding new specialized search features. For example, some engines will allow searching for audio, video, or images. Others have provisions for narrowing the search by date or foreign language. Some allow you to restrict the search by word or phrase filtering. One engine will report results with full or brief descriptions or URL addresses only. Another allows you to limit the number of responses. Almost all provide for advanced searching with special features.

Specialized engines have been developed to search the **"invisible"** or **"deep"** web by going deep into specialty areas such as science, law, and medicine that regular engines may miss. **See page 1-41.**

Most search engines are commercial and profit oriented so their home pages will be filled with advertising, but the searches are usually free.

Click on the **Search Button** of your **ISP's home page.** The **home page** of one of the search engines will open. You can change engines by typing its **URL** in the **Address Box** at the top of the home page and pressing **Enter** or clicking the mouse.

To initiate a simple search, type the **keywords** that represent the concepts of your topic in the blank **Search Box** of the engine and click **Search or Go or whatever term the engine uses.** Remember, you may have to modify your keywords to get the results you want.

> **HINT:** Try each engine in turn to see how it works and compare the results using the same keywords for each engine.

Refining the Search Engine Search

The success of your search depends on four factors:

- **the way the search engine conducts its search**
- **the database of the search engine you are using**
- **your choice of the best keywords**
- **your skill in using the special "operators" for each engine**

The number of web pages added each day is growing astronomically. Because of the vast number of documents available on the Internet, a simple one word query to a search engine can produce thousands of sites each of which has links to others. The result is confusion and frustration because it is impossible for you to examine all of the files.

For example, if you were to enter the key word, Clinton, in the search box, the search engine will produce many documents related to President Clinton, but also many pages for towns named Clinton, inventors named Clinton, schools named Clinton, authors named Clinton and Clintons of every description.

Therefore, you have to use the **special searching rules** of each engine. Being very specific with key words and using **Boolean** and other "operators" will help refine the search.

Some people think **Boolean logic** is a fancy computer term intended to intimidate users. Actually, it is named after the 19th century English mathematician, George Boole, who believed that language could be expressed algebraically. A series of "operators" based on Boolean mathematics is used to refine searches.

Boolean Operators

AND   Use AND between two words. Only files containing both words will appear.

President Clinton AND Gore

OR   Use OR between two words Only files containing at least one of the words will appear.

President Clinton OR Gore

NOT   Use NOT before a word. No files containing the word following NOT will appear.

President Clinton NOT Gore

ALL   is the same as AND

ANY   is the same as OR

Non-Boolean Operators

Some search engines use other non-Boolean operators.

+   is the same as AND. Place the + before the term.

-     is the same as NOT. Place the - before the term.

Proximity Operators

NEAR   Use NEAR between two words. Only files in which the two terms occur within 10 words of each other will appear.

Clinton NEAR Gore

FAR   Use FAR between two words. Only files in which the two terms occur 25 or more words apart will appear.
President Clinton FAR Gore

Phrase Searching Operator

"" Use quotation marks to narrow the search. Bilingual education without the quotation marks will yield many separate files with the word, **education,** and many separate files with **bilingual. Organization names** and **proper names** will work as phrases without quotation marks in some search engines.

Truncation Operator

* Use an asterisk after a root word to generate files with all variations of the word.
human* will yield humans, humanism, humane, etc.

How to Refine Key Words to Improve Your Searches

Step 1. **Examine your topic and identify the key words which are most likely to produce the best results. Try to be as specific as possible.**

Topic: The Impact of Global Warming on Society
Possible Key Words:
global warming

Step 2. **List the possible combinations which may narrow the search and use the appropriate Boolean or other operators.**

Possible Improved Key Words and Phrases:
"global warming" AND causes, "global warming" AND effects, "greenhouse gases" AND "global warming." "global warming" and environment, "global warming AND "U.S.""

If not successful, try different key words. Learn which operators each engine expects. Some engines allow plain language questions, such as **"What are the effects of global warming?"** and give hints for refining the search.

Trouble Shooting Search Problems

Unrelated documents in results?

Use correct spelling of all key words.

Use proper capitalization if engine is case sensitive.

Use the proper syntax for the engine.

Too many documents or documents not related to your topic:

Use Boolean AND to be sure each term appears.

Use Boolean NOT to eliminate irrelevant terms.

Use advanced search procedures of the search engine.

Too few documents:

Use Boolean OR to broaden search.

Use less specific and fewer key words.

Link important terms with Boolean AND.

Use the truncation operator.

Advanced Searching

To refine the original search, most engines will provide forms of **advanced searching** such as **sub-searching** which is a search within the results of a previous search. **Results ranking**, the order in which results appear, is also offered by most engines and also refines the search. Some engines offer **"More like this?"** options to retrieve sites similar to the ones presented. Descriptions of these refinements will usually be found in the **Help,** or **Frequently Asked Questions (FAQ)** sections, or somewhere on the home page of the search engine.

TYPICAL SEARCH ENGINE SEARCH

Just as you did with print material, you must add Internet pages to your bibliography file or Bibliography document in your computer. As you begin your search engine search, get set to make these entries.

Assume you are planning a search for information on **global warming.** You might choose the **AltaVista** search engine that you can open by typing its URL in the address box and clicking. You can find its address on **page 1-40.** When AltaVista opens, you type the keywords, **"global warming"** in the search box. AltaVista will list the first ten sites selected by its system. The illustration on the next page shows the results of the AltaVista search for **global warming.**

AltaVista Search Engine Results for Key Words
"Global Warming"

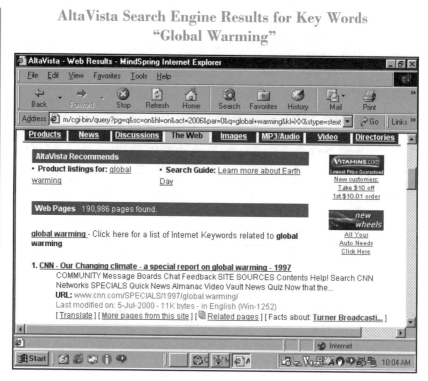

The first thing you should do is print the page in order to compare the results with other search engines and to have a list of sites you may be interested in opening. Searching can get very confusing very quickly if you are not organized.

The illustration above shows only the first of the top 10. You would scroll down for the rest. However, reviewing the page for likely sites you note, just above the first entry, **1. CNN - Our Changing Climate - a special report on global warming -1997,** that AltaVista has a link to a list of **Internet Keywords** related to global warming. You click on it and a list of **keywords** prepared by a company called **RealNames** appears. Finding this link is one example of how you can widen your search as you move through various sites.

You scan the list of keywords on the screen shown on the next page and find the **EPA Global Warming Link** third down from the top on the left side of the page. Since the **Environmental Protection Agency** is a government entity, you decide to begin there, hoping to get some unbiased information. You click on its link. The **EPA Global Warming Home Page** opens as shown in the lower illustration on the next page.

Link to Internet Keywords Related to Global Warming

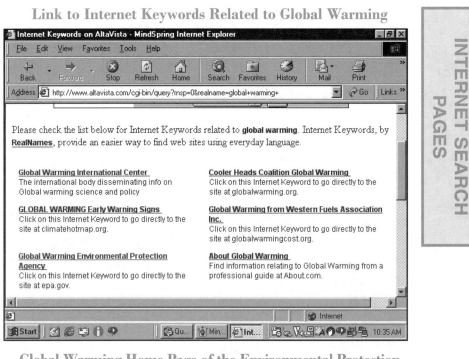

Global Warming Home Page of the Environmental Protection Agency

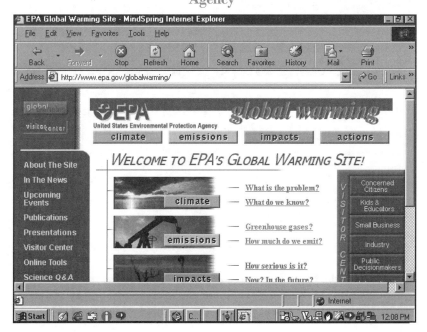

On the **EPA Global Warming Site** you see a link to the question, **"What is the problem?"** and click on it. Another page opens with a discussion of climate. The illustration of the **EPA Climate page** is shown just below. You believe this is a good site for general information on your topic and you decide to prepare a bibliography entry for it. The following paragraphs will explain how to do this job.

Climate Site of the Environmental Protection Agency

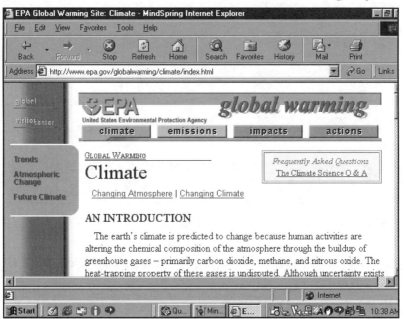

PREPARE INTERNET BIBLIOGRAPHY "CARDS" AND DOWNLOAD DATA TO BIBLIOGRAPHY DOCUMENT

Now that you have located a good source for your paper you must prepare a bibliography "card" or entry and add it to the Bibliography document in your word processor. Follow the directions below:

1. Highlight the **URL** in the address line of the site.
2. Click on **Edit-Copy.**
3. Click on the **Minimize button** in the upper right corner of the screen. The Internet page will close and its icon will jump to the Task Bar.
4. Open the **Bibliography file** in your word processor.
5. Scroll down to the place where you want to position the URL and place the cursor at the spot.

6. Click on **Edit-Paste.** The **URL** will appear in your **Bibliography file** as a **link in color** and **underlined** if you have Windows 98 or later. Any time you are working on your **Bibliography file** in your word processor, clicking on the **URL** will bring up the linked Internet page. Also, any pages that you download will be available offline. You do not have to connect with the Internet unless you want to reach new pages.

7. Return to the **Internet site page** by clicking on the **URL** in your **Bibliography file** or by clicking on the **Internet Page Icon** on the **Task Bar.** Highlight any information you want to copy from the site to the Bibliography entry. Click on **Edit-Copy.**

8. Click on the **Bibliography Icon Tab** in the **Task Bar.** The Bibliography document will open. Position the cursor where you want to paste the information. Click on **Edit-Paste. The highlighted material will be pasted into your Bibliography entry.**

9. Assign the Bibliography entry a **Code number.** Make any **comments** you like to describe the value of the source.

10. Type the **date you accessed** the information from the Internet because it will be needed to prepare the final bibliography.

See the illustration below for the **Bibliography entry** for the **EPA Climate Site** on **page 1-38.** Note the **Code Number, Access Date,** and **Comments** which the student added after copying and pasting the rest of the information.

Bibliography Entry in Student's Computer File
for
EPA Climate Site Shown on Page 38

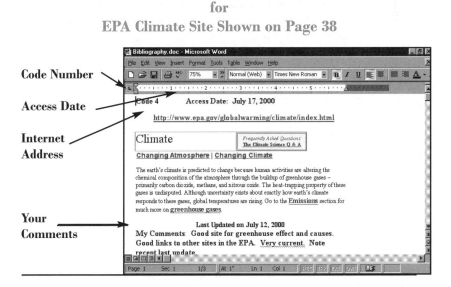

Code Number

Access Date

Internet
Address

Your
Comments

If you stay online, you can go back and forth between your Bibliography file and the Internet by clicking on the minimize button of whichever is open. The minimized file will jump to the Task Bar. Clicking on the minimized button in the Task Bar will bring the page back to the screen.

You can quickly locate several valuable sites and prepare bibliography entries for them using the method described above.

You should also add the URL of good sites to your Bookmark list if you are using Netscape or Favorites list if you are using Internet Explorer. With Internet Explorer do the following:

1. Highlight the URL of the Internet Site.
2. Click on **Favorites** in the **Toolbar**. The dialog box will open.
3. Click on **Add**.
4. Click on **Create New Folder**.
5. Type in the **Folder Name, Bibliography**, and click **OK**.

The folder with the name, **Bibliography,** will appear in the list of favorites. Each time you find a new site of value add it to the Bibliography folder. Netscape users follow similar directions after clicking on Bookmark.

> **HINT: PRINT OUT THE FIRST PAGE** of each search engine's search. Stick with one search engine trying different keywords until you are satisfied that you have exhausted all possibilities. Try each search engine in turn using its special search rules and compare the results.

POPULAR SEARCH ENGINES

AltaVista
http://www.altavista.com

Go
http://www.go.com

Lycos
http://www.lycos.com

Yahoo
http://www.yahoo.com

Excite
http://www.excite.com

Hotbot
http://www.hotbot.com

Webcrawler
> **http://www.webcrawler.com**

Northern Light
> **http://www.northernlight.com**

Google
> **http://www.google.com**

Fast Search
> **http://ussc.alltheweb.com**

Atomica
> **http://www.atomica.com**

GoTo
> **http://www.goto.com**

About
> **http://www.about.com**

SEARCH 2: SEARCH THE INVISIBLE WEB

The **"visible web"** is searched by the popular search engines listed above.   The **"invisible web"** consists primarily of thousands of specialized databases that cannot be reached by conventional search engines. You must go to a page with a search box for the specialized database you are seeking.

POPULAR INVISIBLE WEB SEARCH ENGINES

Invisible Web
> **http://www.invisibleweb.com**

Academicinfo
> **http://www.academicinfo.net**

Alpha Search
> **http://www.calvin.edu/library/searreso/internet/as**

Infomine Multiple Database Search
> **http://infomine.ucr.edu/search.phtml**

WebData
> **http://webdata.com**

Biolinks
> **http://www.biolinks.com**

Completeplanet
> **http:www//completeplanet.com**

The Big Hub
> **http://www.thebighub.com**

SEARCH 3: SEARCH META-SEARCH ENGINES

Meta-search engines search several engines at the same time and display the results from all of the engines searched. However, meta-search engines differ in the way they report the results of searches. Some list the results by individual search engine in sequence while others provide a single list. One permits the user to sort results by domain while others offer other options for reporting results.

Meta-search engines also differ in the way they search and in the special instructions you must give them so you will have to study the **sites** carefully.

POPULAR META-SEARCH ENGINES

Dogpile

    http://www.dogpile.com

Inference Find

    http://www.inference.com/infind

MetaCrawler

    http://www.metacrawler.com

Ixquick

    http://www.ixquick.com

Ask Jeeves

    http://askjeeves.com

SEARCH 4: SEARCH SUBJECT DIRECTORIES

Many universities, libraries, search engine companies and other organizations are producing subject directories. Directories range widely in quality and content. Some are carefully evaluated by experts who write annotations while others are not very scholarly.

Directories may lead you to sources you may not have known existed. For example, you may find journals and magazines, organizations, and even full text material related to your subject.

Subject directories are usually organized like the branches of a tree so the user can search from general to increasingly more specific topics. As with search engines, read any **Help, FAQ,** or other searching tips of the directory sites carefully to get clear directions.

Each subject directory will look different but, in general, you will see a list of major topics on its home page. For example, the **Yahoo** home page has a directory which begins with **Arts and Humanities, Business, Computers, Education,** etc. If you were searching for information on **welfare reform**, clicking on **Sociology** under the **Social Science** heading and entering **"welfare reform"** in the search box would yield a list of sites along with links to other sites.

> **HINT:** Just as with search engines, it is a good idea to try each directory, locate valuable sources, and add them to your Favorites or Bookmark list.

POPULAR SUBJECT DIRECTORIES

Search Engines
http://www.search engine name.com

Excite
http://excite.com

Google
http://www.google.com

Yahoo
http://www.yahoo.com

Argus: The Clearing House
http://www.clearinghouse.net

WWW Virtual Library
http://www.vlib.org

INFOMINE: Scholarly Internet Resource Collections
http://infomine.ucr.edu

Librarians' Index to the Internet
http://www.lii.org

UCB Library and Internet Resources by Subject
http://lib.berkeley.edu

POPULAR SUBJECT DIRECTORIES, continued

Scout Report Signpost
> **http://www.signpost.org/signpost**

Britannica Internet Guide
> **http://www.ebig.com**

BUBL Link
> **http://www.bubl.ac.uk**

Magellan
> **http:www.mckinley.com**

Open Directory
> **http://www.dmoz.org**

LookSmart
> **http://www.looksmart.com**

SEARCH 5: SEARCH GUIDES TO PERIODICALS

Just as you used the print copy of the *Readers' Guide to Periodicals* in the library, you can use several online periodical guides to find magazines or journals related to your subject. Some magazines and journals provide indexes to their publications. You also may be able to access full text articles from magazines or journals. Several journals are now published in **electronic journal format (ejournals)** for easy retrieval. However, some journals are available only to students at university libraries or require subscriptions.

Continuing a search for information on **welfare reform**, you might open the **Excite** search engine. If you type **"welfare reform" AND journals** in the search box, many sites will appear.

POPULAR GUIDES TO PERIODICALS

Many journals and magazines have their own home pages.
> **http://www.title of magazine or journal**

Use a search engine with a key word search
> **Type: The name of the periodical in the search box and click search.**
> > **or**
> **Type the subject AND journals or periodicals in the search box and click Search.**

POPULAR GUIDES TO PERIODICALS, continued

Use a search engine subject directory
> **Click on a subject such as "Business" and type the word, journals, in the search box and click Search.**

Use one of the following Internet periodical guides.

Ecola Newstand
> **http://www.ecola.com**

Internet Public Library Reading Room Newspapers
> **http:www.ipl.org/reading/news**

Internet Public Library Reading Room Serials
> **http:www.ipl.org/reading/serials**

UC San Diego Library of Directories of Electronic Journals
> **http://libraries.ucsd.edu/ejournals.html**

SEARCH GUIDES TO BOOKS

SEARCH 6: SEARCH GUIDES TO BOOKS

Although the Internet has no catalog, a few Internet sites are beginning to catalog books. Full text is available at some sites. Each site has different resources and each has different rules for accessing material.

The **Internet Public Library,** for example, offers searching by **Dewey Decimal Classification** as well as searching by author and title as in a conventional library. Clicking on the **300 Social Sciences** classification, and narrowing the classification to **362.5** will produce possible sources for the topic, **Welfare Reform.**

POPULAR GUIDES TO BOOKS

College or University Libraries
> **http://Internet address of college or university. edu**
> The home page may contain links to the library and then to collections of books.

Internet Public Library Reading Room Texts
> **http:www.ipl.org/reading/books**

POPULAR GUIDES TO BOOKS, continued

Literature Online
http://lion.chadwyck.com

Digital Books, Images, and More
http://sunsite.berkeley.edu/Collections

Online Books Page
http://www.digital.library.upenn.edu/books

SEARCH 7. SEARCH LIBRARIES AND LIBRARY REFERENCES

Many university and other major libraries allow users to access their catalogs via the Internet. Some enable you to download text. The following sites will provide information on libraries and their collections.

POPULAR LIBRARY GUIDES

Search Engines
Type: libraries in the search box and click search

Libweb
http://sunsite.berkeley.edu/Libweb

Internet Public Library
http://www.ipl.org

Library of Congress
http://www.lcweb.loc.gov

SEARCH 8: SEARCH ACADEMIC MAILING LISTS IN LISTSERVS

Many academic organizations conduct discussions on specific subjects. You may find information by locating a mailing list which deals with your subject. There are a number of mailing list finders, but as with search engines each differs in the manner in which it searches. Read the **Help** files for specific instructions.

POPULAR LISTSERV MAILING LIST GUIDES

For a print book with the addresses of listservs, see the *Directory of Electronic Journals, Newsletters and Academic Discussion Groups* by Lisbeth King, Diane Kovacs, and others.

POPULAR LISTSERV MAILING LIST GUIDES, continued

Search Engines

> **Type: listservs or listservs AND your subject in the search box
> and click Search.**

Kovacs Directory of Scholarly E-lists
> **http://n2h2.com/KOVACS/Sindex.html**

Liszt

> **http://www.liszt.com**

Catalist

> **http://www.lsoft.com/lists/listref.html**

To Subscribe to a Mailing List

1. Open your Internet connection. Click on your E-mail
   software.
2. Click on New Message. The message box will appear.
3. Type the listserv subscription address at the To: prompt.
4. Tab down to the message area. Type SUBSCRIBE (name
   of listserv)(your name). Click Send.

To Send a Message to a Listserv

1. Obtain the mail address of the mailing list. It is usually
   different from the subscription address.
2. Follow the above directions for subscribing, except type
   the message you want to send in the message area.

To Unsubscribe from a Mailing List

1. Follow the instructions for subscribing above except type
   SIGNOFF (mailing list subscribe address).

SEARCH 9: SEARCH E-MAIL SOURCES

You may want to locate an important researcher or source for your
research. You can use one of the E-mail address finders below.

POPULAR E-MAIL ADDRESS GUIDES

Bigfoot

> **http://www.bigfoot.com**

Four 11

> **http://www.four11.com**

SEARCH 10: SEARCH USENET NEWSGROUPS

Newsgroups use electronic bulletin boards to exchange messages about many topics. While most are not scholarly, a few academic forums do exist. Be extremely cautious before accepting and citing any information received from a newsgroup or chat room. Newgroups can be accessed on the Web, but Listservs are accessed through E-mail.

You may need special software which many ISPs now provide to access newsgroups or chat rooms. Methods for accessing newsgroups vary. Use the **Help** file of your ISP or search engine.

POPULAR USENET FINDERS

Use a search engine.

> **Type: Newsgroups, Usenet, or Newsgroups AND your subject in the search box and click Search.**

Groups.google
> **http://groups.google.com**

EVALUATING INTERNET SOURCES

Information which appears in print form has usually been subjected to careful editing based on long established journalistic standards. Print publishers are usually diligent in checking the facts in articles which they publish. The editors of scholarly journals are most judicious in selecting and editing research articles. Nevertheless, the careful researcher will scrupulously evaluate print material for accuracy, point of view, and bias.

If print material needs careful evaluation, information obtained on the Internet needs even more intensive scrutiny before being accepted. Responsible online publishers and writers maintain the same standards as those for print media, but others may not. With very little expense anyone can become an electronic publisher, set up a home page, write articles for Usenet or Listserv discussion groups, send E-mail, and enter chat rooms. In many cases, it is impossible to determine exactly who the writer is or whom he or she represents. As you obtain information, use the Internet Source Evaluation Checklist on the next page to screen material.

INTERNET SOURCE EVALUATION CHECKLIST

Site **Edu, org, gov,** or **mil** sites maintained by colleges and universities, professional organizations, military, and government agencies are most reliable. Be cautious of **com** sites that are usually filled with advertising and may contain information for which payment has been made for publication. Check **Listservs** carefully and be wary of **Usenet** discussion groups and **chat rooms.** **E-mail** should be carefully evaluated and accepted only if it is a personal communication from an expert.

Author Is the author **well-known, expert, qualified**? Is there an **association** with an established, recognized institution? Enter only the first part of the URL and domain name to bring up the organization's home page to find out about the author's association.

Publisher Is the publisher an establishment such as a **university, professional organization, government agency**, or **well-known publisher**? Be careful of publishers that exist only on the Web. Check these judiciously. Find out who they are and their qualifications to publish on the subject. Look at the **bottom of the page** or click on **"About Us"** or **"Contact Us"** to learn more about the source. You may find an **e-mail address**.

Links Do **hypertext links** take you to **educational** or other solid sites which can lead to further reliable research and not to commercial sites?

Bibliography Is there a **bibliography** which attests to scholarship and leads to quality sources?

References Are **quality sources** cited which you can locate and check?

Currency Is information current with **recent publication date**? Internet documents are frequently updated. Look for the date the material was last updated at the bottom. of the page.

Point of View   Are **facts** rather than **opinion** presented? Much on the Internet is highly opinionated without grounding in fact. Is the author's **point of view** clear and supported by facts? Is the author's **purpose** to persuade, explain, or inform? Is the source a political, activist, or commercial lobby whose goal is to influence public opinion and legislation?

Audience   Is information intended for **mature, serious readers**? Reject material that is frivolous or chatty.

DETERMINE THE SIGNIFICANT ISSUES OF YOUR TOPIC BY REVIEWING YOUR PRELIMINARY RESEARCH

After researching several articles in magazines, journals, books, and the Internet and collecting many bibliography entries, you should have a much clearer idea of the significant issues related to your topic. Look through the notes on your bibliography cards and/or Bibliography file in your computer and/or computer printouts.

What are the points of view? Are there many or just a few? Are there major controversies? What aspect of the subject do you want to explore? Jot down a few ideas. Then set the material aside for a day and let the information percolate in your mind.

DECIDE HOW YOU WILL DEAL WITH THE TOPIC

Now is the time to bring your own ideas into the project. Through your reading of sources have you developed your own point of view? Do you agree or disagree with your sources? Has some new or original approach leaped into your mind? Could you apply the information in the sources in a new way? What do you think about this topic?

Go back to the prewriting exercises described on **page 1-3** and do them again, this time with the new information you have garnered. Do some free writing, answer the 5W's and H questions, and try mapping your ideas. Write down your thoughts. Let them flow. This is the most important part of the research paper project because it will lead directly to your writing the **THESIS STATEMENT** in Task 4.

Time for Task 3: 5-8 hours

TASK 4: DEVELOP A THESIS STATEMENT

This task is to refine your ideas and develop a thesis which can be "proved" or supported by your research. Read through the following list of Thesis Approaches to see which fits your thinking. You may want to re-read the entries in your computer Bibliography file and/or your bibliography cards and/or printouts once more. Note that the thesis examples are all in declarative sentences which can be "proved" with facts.

THESIS APPROACHES

Chronology---	**The rise of the Imagist Movement can be traced over a period of twenty years.**
Procedure---	**Five steps are required to produce liquid oxygen.**
Cause/Effect---	**Economic factors caused deterioration in Sino-Soviet relations in 1950.**
Problem---	**Differing Moslem ideologies make Israeli-Palestinian peace difficult.**
Solution---	**The energy crisis can be solved by solar and nuclear power.**
Comparison---	**Acupuncture is a better anesthetic than malothane.**
Similarity---	**TV and motion picture writing are similar in several respects.**
Difference---	**Marriage rites differ among Far Eastern, Middle Eastern and Western families.**
Relationship---	**Hemingway's life experiences influenced his work.**
Analysis---	**Three major issues are related to the crisis in North Korea.**
Literary Theme---	**Romantic themes prevail in two major works of William Wordsworth.**
Pro---	**Kennedy's handling of the Cuban missile crisis was good foreign policy.**
Con---	**Four medical theories oppose radical mastectomy in breast cancer.**
Category---	**Several ethnic populations in America grew during the past ten years.**

Now write your thesis statement in a declarative sentence. Identify which thesis approach you are using. Think the words, "I believe..." just before you write your thesis statement. This will insure that **YOU** and **YOUR** ideas are in the paper. Check your thesis against the following checklist.

THESIS CHECKLIST

My thesis statement is:
(I believe)_____

My thesis statement:

■ uses the (select from the list above) thesis approach.
■ is not too broad.
■ is not too narrow or technical unless required.
■ can be proved with the material I have found.
■ is scholarly.
■ is OK with my instructor.

If your thesis statement meets all the above criteria, go on to **Task 5**. If not, return to **Task 4** and write a new thesis statement.

Time for Task 4: 1-2 Hours

TASK 5: WRITE A TOPIC OUTLINE

This task helps you organize the information you have found to prove your thesis statement. The thesis approach will suggest the outline. **Type the outline in the computer in a document named, Topic Outline or write in longhand.**

OUTLINING HINTS

Organize and classify ideas under major headings which support and prove the thesis statement. Do not include your introduction and conclusion in this outline. They will be written as part of **Task 9**.

Plan at least two subdivisions under each major heading. If you cannot, your outline is faulty. Subheads should also have at least two subdivisions.

Use the Harvard outline style or the more modern decimal outline style in which all information introduced by the same first numeral relates to the same major topic.

HARVARD OUTLINE	DECIMAL OUTLINE
I.	1.
A.	1. 1.
B.	1. 2.
1.	1. 2. 1.
2.	1. 2. 2.
a.	1. 2. 2. 1.

SAMPLE OUTLINES

DIFFERENCE THESIS APPROACH

If you selected this approach, you have to identify the elements which differ and then show how they differ.

Thesis Statement: *Marriage rites differ among Far Eastern, Middle Eastern, and Western Families.*

1. **Marriage Rites in the Far East**
   - 1. 1. **Vows**
   - 1. 2. **Dowries**
   - 1. 3. **Clothing**
   - 1. 4. **Ceremonies**
2. **Marriage Rites in the Middle East**
   - 2. 1. **Vows**
   - 2. 2. **Etc.**

LITERARY THEMES THESIS APPROACH

If you selected this approach, you must identify the literary themes and then show how they appear in the author's works.

Thesis Statement: *Romantic themes prevail in two major works of Wordsworth.*

1. **Romantic themes**
   - 1. 1. **Return to nature**
   - 1. 2. **Sympathy with humble**
   - 1. 3. **Escape from convention**
2. **Themes in Wordsworth's works**
   - 2. 1. **"Tintern Abbey"**
     - 2. 1. 1. **Samples of return to nature**
     - 2. 1. 2. **Samples of sympathy with humble**
     - 2. 1. 3. **Samples of escape from convention**
   - 2. 2. **"Intimations of Immortality**
     - 2. 2. 1. **Etc.**

Time for Task 5: 1-3 Hours

TASK 6: CHANGE TOPIC OUTLINE TO A SENTENCE OUTLINE

The next task is to change your **Topic Outline** to a **Sentence Outline** in preparation for writing. Each topic should be transformed into a topic sentence around which your paragraphs will be constructed. Remember, a topic sentence is like a little thesis statement. Each topic sentence must be supported or "proved" by the paragraph which follows it. The example below based on the Wordsworth outline on the previous page shows how the topics are expanded into declarative sentence.

Open the **Topic Outline document** and **Save** it as **Sentence Outline**. Now open both documents and **split them horizontally** with the **Windows menu**. Look at the **topic outline** and write the **sentence outline** in the **Sentence Outline document**.

Thesis Statement: **Romantic themes prevail in two major works of Wordsworth.**

TOPIC OUTLINE	SENTENCE OUTLINE
1. Romantic Themes	1. Romanticism is associated with several themes which set it apart from neo-Classicism.
1. 1. Return to nature	1. 1. A return to nature and its beauty characterize the Romantic movement.
1. 2. Sympathy with with humble	1. 2. The simplicity of the rustic life attracted many Romantic poets.

Time for Task 6: 1-5 Hours

TASK 7: CLASSIFY NOTE SOURCES TO MATCH SENTENCE OUTLINE

ORGANIZE BIBLIOGRAPHY ENTRIES

This task is to arrange the information from all of your sources to match your sentence outline. Go back through your **bibliography entries** of all types: **3x5 cards, library online catalog printouts,** and your own **computer Bibliography file.**

Assume that you are writing on Wordsworth and the first sentence in your outline is: **Romanticism is associated with several themes which set it apart from neo-Classicism.** You must look for all the bibliography entries which contain information on the themes of the Romantic movement and information on neo-Classicism.

Begin by printing your **computer Bibliography file** and cutting up the entries into individual **bibliography "cards."** Put them in a pile with your **3x5 handwritten bibliography cards** and any **printouts from online library sources** you obtained.

Each **card, computer file,** or **printout** should have a **call number, location, page numbers, Internet URL and access date if applicable,** and **your personal comment.** Read the comments you wrote on each "card" to identify the sources with information about the first topic sentence dealing with Romantic themes and neo-Classicism.

Next, you must retrieve the actual sources represented by the bibliography entries to read the material and evaluate it for possible use to support the first topic sentence.

FOR PRINT MATERIAL:

Return to the library stacks or reference desk with all of the bibliography cards or printouts that refer to print material in books, journals, reference guides, etc. Find the books, journals, magazines, or reference books with information on the first topic sentence. Refer to the page number(s) on the bibliography entries and re-read the pages. Identify those sources which you can use to support the first topic sentence of your outline.

Go to the photocopy machine in your library. Most charge only 10 or 15 cents per page. At that rate you can copy 100 pages for $10.00 or $15.00 which may well be worth it. Copy all the pages you need from each book or journal.

On the top edge of each photocopy write your bibliography entry code number, the page number(s), and outline topic sentence. You will need the code number to find the bibliography card entry with the full bibliographic information when you prepare the **Works Cited** or **Reference lists** at the end of your paper. Continue this process until you have photocopied and classified all the print material that relates to the first topic sentence.

FOR PRINTOUTS OF LIBRARY ONLINE SOURCES:

Find the printouts of **microforms, abstracts** or **full text articles** which relate to the first topic sentence. Identify those sources which you can use to support the first topic sentence of your outline. **On the top edge of each printout write your bibliography entry code number, the page number(s), and outline topic sentence.**

FOR PRINTOUTS OF INTERNET PAGES

Find the printouts of **Internet pages** that relate to the first topic sentence. Identify those sources that you can use to support the first topic sentence of your outline. Go online, open the Internet pages, and highlight relevant material. **Copy-Paste** the material into your computer **Sentence Outline** under the first topic sentence. Tag each with its **bibliography code number, topic sentence, URL** and access date, and any **other bibliographic data** required.

SUMMARIZE, PARAPHRASE OR QUOTE THE SOURCES

You should have all the information related to the first topic sentence. You now must decide how you will incorporate the source material into your paper. Each source will have to be summarized, paraphrased, or quoted. Of course, credit must be given to each source through a correct citation. The following instructions illustrate the three techniques.

Look at the illustration below which represents a photocopy of a page from the book, *William Wordsworth*, published by Twayne Publishers, Inc. Assume that you found this passage and intend to use it in your paper to support the topic sentence, **2. 1. 1. The Romantic theme, a return to nature, is clearly seen in "Tintern Abbey."** By writing, **paraphrase, quote,** or **summarize** on the photocopy you would tell **yourself how you plan to use the material in the text of your paper.**

Code Number

Topic Sentence

How you plan to use
the source.

③ *Romantic theme, a return to nature, is seen in "Tintern Abbey"*

Paraphrase

Its repetitive words phrases, and patterns give to the flowing rhythms a wonderfully resonant and noble beauty. The poetic expression of the impact of the scenic landscape upon the innermost recesses of the poet's mind was as spontaneous as it was powerful. The poem took shape while his feelings were overflowing with excess of joy and while his faith in the power of nature to dispel "fear or pain or grief" was still at high tide. In after years he qualified and subdued his pronouncements in "Tintern Abbey' But he never lost delight in the simple converse of Nature or his faith that all created things can bring pleasure to the sensitive person impelled by love or praise.

HOW TO SUMMARIZE OR PARAPHRASE OR QUOTE

SUMMARY: **Author's ideas in your words in shortened version**

Directions: Read the passage. Do not look at it again. Rewrite in your own words without your ideas or interpretation. Read the original again to check for accuracy.

> The rhythm and phrasing of "Tintern Abbey" reflect the strong feeling developed in Wordsworth as he reacted to Nature's landscapes. Later, his belief in the power of nature was less fervent, although he always loved the simple joys it brought.

PARAPHRASE: **Author's ideas in your words with no attempt to shorten.**

Directions: Read passage. Do not look at it again. Rewrite in your own words without your ideas or interpretation, but do not shorten. Make author's ideas simpler. Read the original again to check for accuracy.

> "Tintern Abbey" reflects the powerful emotions of near ecstasy Wordsworth felt at the time. The poem's content and form are an outgrowth of the effect of the natural landscape on the poet and his belief that nature could shield humankind from the sadness and pain of life. As he grew older he was less enthusiastic about the ability of nature to soothe the trouble spirit. Nevertheless, he continued to derive joy from communing with nature.

QUOTATION: **Author's words exactly.**

Directions: Using quotation marks, copy the passage exactly including punctuation, underlining, etc. Even errors should be copied and followed with the Latin word, [sic], "thus," in brackets and underlined.

"Its repetitive words, phrases, and patterns give to the flowing rhythms a wonderfully resonant and noble beauty. the poetic expression of the impact of the scenic landscape upon the innermost recesses of the poet's mind was as spontaneous as it was powerful."

PLAGIARISM

Plagiarism is the improper use of another's ideas or language. Paraphrasing without giving credit or using original phrases or words without quotation marks are definitely examples of plagiarism. Academic and legal penalties are severe and can include a failing grade, expulsion, or denial of a college degree. Be scholarly and honest.

WRITE PARAPHRASE, SUMMARY, OR QUOTE NOTES DIRECTLY IN YOUR OUTLINE

Open your Outline document. Locate the first topic sentence in the outline. Take out the photocopied sources which relate to the topic sentence. Decide whether you will paraphrase, summarize, or quote the source and type it directly under the topic sentence. Try not to have more than two or three sources to support any one topic sentence. Add its code number and page number(s) and a note stating the whether it is quote, paraphrase or summary. Change the Internet material already in the outline to quotes, paraphrases, or summaries. Just below is an illustration of a student's paraphrase of the paragraph on "Tintern Abbey" in his or her Outline document.

Student's Paraphrase of Note in Outline Document

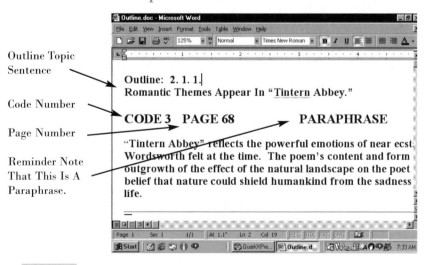

Outline Topic Sentence

Code Number

Page Number

Reminder Note That This Is A Paraphrase.

Outline: 2. 1. 1.
Romantic Themes Appear In "Tintern Abbey."

CODE 3   PAGE 68   PARAPHRASE

"Tintern Abbey" reflects the powerful emotions of near ecst Wordsworth felt at the time. The poem's content and form outgrowth of the effect of the natural landscape on the poet belief that nature could shield humankind from the sadness life.

OUTLINING IN LONGHAND

If you are writing in longhand, use large foolscap pads. Write each topic sentence of your outline on a separate sheet. Write the paraphrase, quote, or summary on a 5 x 8 inch card with the topic sentence, code number, page number(s) and any other bibliographic data needed at the top. Clip the card(s) to the sheet. See the illustration below.

5 x 8 Inch Note Card With Paraphrase

Code ③ 2.1.1. Romantic theme, return to nature, appears in "Tintern Abbey"

PARAPHRASE

"Tintern Abbey" reflects the powerful emotions of near ecstasy Wordsworth felt at the time. The poem's content and form are an outgrowth of the effect of the natural landscape on the poet and his belief that nature could shield human kind from the sadness and pain of life. As he grew older he was less enthusiastic about the ability of nature to soothe the troubled spirit. Nevertheless, he continued to derive joy from communing with nature.

When finished, all of your sources will have been paraphrased, quoted, or summarized and arranged with the topic sentences in your outline.

TASK 8: WRITE THE FIRST DRAFT

This task is to flesh out your outline. At this point read through your outline and sources and think about how you will draft your paper. Begin with the first topic sentence in your outline. Decide, in general, how you will use the various paraphrases, quotes, and summaries in your outline to support the topic sentences. Think about maintaining unity of thought by making certain that each source pertains to the topic sentence and helps to "prove" it.

PARAGRAPH BUILDING

You can use your paraphrases, quotes, and summaries as **examples, definitions, explanations, statistical data, comparisons, or details,** to support your topic sentences. For example, if your topic sentence contains a somewhat unusual or new concept to your reader, you would use one of your sources as an explanation to help clarify the concept.

Proceed with each topic sentence. Reread the sources. Be creative in your plan to use them. Each paragraph should be about one major idea which is expressed in its topic sentence. However, each paragraph must also be a building block which supports the main thesis and gives the paper coherence.

While you will rely heavily on your research sources, be sure the major thesis and thrust of your paper is your own. Remember to keep saying, "I believe..." about your thesis to be sure you do not just cut and paste the ideas of other.

DECIDE ON A CITATION STYLE - MLA OR APA

Before you begin to write, decide with your instructor whether you will be using the Modern Language Association or American Psychological Association style of citation.

WRITING WITH COMPUTER NOTES

Open a new document and save it with the title of your paper. This will be your research paper. Open the Outline document which now contains all of your paraphrases, summaries, and quotes under each topic sentence. Your Research Paper document and the Outline document will both be open. Split the documents horizontally with the Windows menu. Both documents will be displayed. See the illustration on the next page.

Begin writing in your Research Paper document. When you want to place a paraphrase, quote or summary in your paper, select the text in the Outline document and choose **Copy** from the **Edit** menu. Click in your Research Paper document window and move the cursor to the place where you want to insert the material. Choose **Paste** from the **Edit** menu and the text will be inserted. Revise the text to insert the parenthetical citation in smooth and fluent language. Review **pages 4-2** to **4-4** for the **MLA style** or **pages 9-2** to **9-3** for the **APA style.**

Temporarily type the bibliography entry code number near each paraphrase, summary, or quote so you can cite the sources accurately in the Works Cited or References list later.

Writing With a Split Screen
The Outline Document Is Above the Research Paper. The Writer Can Copy the Paraphrase in The Outline Document and Paste It in the Research Paper Document

Outline Document

Outline.doc - Microsoft Word

File Edit View Insert Format Tools Table Window Help

80%   Normal   Times New Roman   **B** *I* U

Topic Sentence
Code Number
Paraphrase

Outline: 2. 1. 1.
Romantic Themes Appear In "Tintern Abbey."
CODE 3   PAGE 68   PARAPHRASE
"Tintern Abbey" reflects the powerful emotions of near ecstasy
Wordsworth felt at the time. The poem's content and form are an

Page 1   Sec 1   1/1   At 1"   Ln 1   Col 1   REC TRK EXT OVR

Research Paper Document

Research Paper.doc - Microsoft Word

File Edit View Insert Format Tools Table Window Help

80%   Body Text   Times New Roman   **B** *I* U

Topic Sentence
Code & Page #

Paraphrase

Research Paper: Draft
The Romantic theme, "return to nature" appears in "Tintern Abbey"
Code 3   Page 68
"Tintern Abbey" reflects the powerful emotions of near ecstasy
Wordsworth felt at the time. The poem's content and form are an

Page 1   Sec 1   1/1   At 1.2"   Ln 2   Col 10   REC TRK EXT OVR

Start

WRITING WITH LONGHAND NOTE CARDS

If you used the longhand method of note taking, you now have a collection of note cards containing your summaries, paraphrases, and quotes clipped to your longhand foolscap pad outline. Begin writing in longhand or on the word processor. If you are writing in long hand, you can simply staple the cards directly to the pages of the first draft at the places where you want them to appear. Draw lines across the paper above and below the source to set it off.

If you are using the word processor, you can type your quotes, paraphrases, and summaries into your paper at the appropriate points. Temporarily type the bibliography entry code number near each paraphrase, summary, or quote so you can cite the sources accurately in the Works Cited or References list later. Revise the text to insert the parenthetical citation in smooth and fluent language. Review **pages 4-2 to 4-4** for the **MLA style** or **pages 9-2 to 9-3** for the **APA style.**

BEGIN WRITING IN EARNEST

Do not write the introduction or conclusion at this time. Write quickly and do not focus too heavily on grammar and style for now. Your goal is to get your thesis proved by getting your ideas and your research down on paper. Remember to put yourself into the project. The paper must reflect you and your thesis.

Writing in the third person only, begin with the first topic sentence in your sentence outline and write the sentences that prove it. Quotations should comprise no more than one fifth of the paper. Plan to have no more than four citations per page. As you include your sources, be sure to write the parenthetical citations for each using the formats in either **Chapter 4 or Chapter 9.**

Write the transitional sentences which tie the researched material together. Work straight through to the end and put your paper aside for a day when you finish.

TASK 9: REVISE THE FIRST DRAFT

Print the first draft. Read your paper for content only. Note errors and ideas for changes in the margin. Rewrite, delete, move text, cut and paste on your computer. If you are using longhand, cross out, and draw arrows to show where to move text. Insert new text between the lines. Use the **Content Checklist** on the next page to be sure your paper is okay. Ask someone else to read your paper to see if it meets all the criteria.

CONTENT CHECKLIST

- Thesis is clearly stated
- Paper is logically developed
- Paper follows outline
- Thesis is proved
- Sources are cited
- Plagiarism checked
- Your ideas apparent
- Good transitional paragraphs

WRITE THE INTRODUCTION

Tell why you wrote the paper. Describe the positions others have taken on the subject. State your thesis and tell how you approached the subject. Explain the major points in the paper. Discuss the reasons why your reader should be interested in the topic.

WRITE THE CONCLUSION

Restate the thesis. Summarize the ideas and arguments presented. Explain your conclusions. Discuss leads to further investigation. Tell why you think the topic is important, interesting and worthwhile.

CHECK FOR GRAMMAR AND STYLE

Reread the paper for grammar and style. Use your word processor's spell check and grammar check features if available. Make corrections as needed. Use the grammar and style checklist on the next page to be sure your paper is perfect.

Review **Chapter 2** with particular attention to improving writing style by varying sentence openings, sentence lengths, and avoiding passive voice. Plan interesting and smooth transitions between sentences and paragraphs. Avoid wordiness, jargon, slang, or colloquial language. Remember to eliminate bias when referring to ethnic groups, gender, and socioeconomic classes. Use the **Grammar and Style Checklist** on the next page to be sure everything is in order.

GRAMMAR AND STYLE CHECKLIST

- Clear topic sentences
- Topic sentences proved
- No fragments or run-ons
- Good paragraph transitions
- Consistent tense used
- Subjects and verbs agree
- Pronouns and antecedents agree

- No misplaced modifiers
- Strong verbs and nouns
- Language fluent
- Varied sentence openings
- Spelling correct
- Third person used
- Parallel structure used

Time For Task 9: 3-6 Hours

TASK 10: PREPARE THE WORKS CITED OR REFERENCE LIST

Carefully read the instructions for the **MLA Works Cited** list on **page 4-5** or for the **APA Reference** list on **page 9-4**. Alphabetize your bibliography cards and entries. Check the format for each source in the sample pages. Type and paginate the pages as required.

Time for Task 10: 2 Hours

TASK 11: TYPE THE FINAL DRAFT

Rewrite the paper including all revisions, deletions, and additions. Pay careful attention to the format of title pages, margins, pagination, citation technique, and especially, the method of preparing the Works Cited list or Reference list. Styles vary with regard to the handling of quotations so be extra careful and follow the appropriate styles.

Find the chapter with specific instructions for your word processor for details on these matters. Setting up the pages can be a bit tricky, especially with regard to pagination.

Print your paper on good quality, 8 and 1/2 x 11 inch paper on a letter quality printer or better. After printing the paper, proofread carefully again for omitted words, punctuation, spelling and grammatical errors. You should now have a paper which you can present to your instructor with pride.

Congratulations! Hope it earns an A+! You deserve it.

Time for Task 11: 4-8 Hours

Proofreading:
A Writing Review

Your paper should contain no spelling, punctuation, or grammatical errors and conform to the standards of usage and style established by the Modern Language Association and American Psychological Association. Language should be non-sexist and free of bias of any kind. This chapter provides a review of these language elements as well as suggestions for improving sentence and writing style.

LANGUAGE MECHANICS

PUNCTUATION

USE COMMAS

- Before *and, but, for,* and *nor* between independent clauses.
  > The judge approved the verdict, **but** the appeals court reversed it.

- Between *words, phrases,* and *clauses* in series.
  > We assembled **men, women, girls**, and **boys**.

- Between *adjectives* that modify the *same noun.*
  > The flat tax will create **new, unusual** hardships.

- To set off parenthetical comments.
  > Exercising, **however,** is not the only way to lose weight.

- To set off words which, if omitted, would not change the meaning of the sentence.
  > Frank Sinatra, **one of the most popular singers of the twentieth century,** will present a concert Tuesday evening.

- To set off clauses beginning with *which, whom, whose, who,* and *that,* which if omitted, would not change the meaning of the sentence.

    The Boeing 747, **which has one of the best safety records,** was responsible for the boom in intercontinental travel.

- After a long introductory clause or phrase.

    If we learn the cause of the expansion, we will be in a position to make better decisions.

USE SEMICOLONS

- Between independent clauses without a conjunction.

    The men in the study were young; **the women were old.**

- To separate items in a series when the items are separated by commas.

    Speakers included **Mr. Jones, the teacher; Ms. Crashet, the principal; and Dr. Rogers, the superintendent.**

USE COLONS

- To introduce a list.

    The following members will attend the convention: **Robertson, Bohannon, and Rabinowitz.**

- To separate a complete, independent clause and a second clause which illustrates or elaborates the first. If the second is a complete sentence it begins with a capital.

    The story is a complete fabrication: **The brothers invented the entire scenario to protect each other.**

USE DASHES

- To show a sharp break in the continuity of a sentence. Use two hyphens, but use sparingly.

    Jim saw himself as handsome--**others saw him as conceited**--and played the role.

USE PARENTHESES

· To show an even sharper break in the continuity of a sentence than the use of dashes.

The New York art scene *(for some the epitome of hypocrisy)* is alway lively.

USE BRACKETS

· To enclose a parenthesis within a parenthesis.

(The Lenape tribe *[1710]* was part of the Iroquois group).

USE HYPHENS

Use a good dictionary as a guide, but in general use hyphens:

· In *compound adjectives* beginning with adverbs *ill, better, best, little,* or *well.*
better-dressed, ill-prepared, little-used, best-known, well-loved

· In *compound adjectives* which *precede a noun* but not in adjectives beginning with an adverb ending in *-ly.*
slow-moving vehicles, but not *freshly minted money*

· Do not use after prefixes: *after, anti, bi, counter, mid, mini, multi, non, over, pre, pro, semi, socio, sub, super, ultra, under.*
aftereffects, antifreeze, bipolar, counterattack, miniskirt, multinational, nonjudgemental, overpaid, preschool, profile, semicircular, socioeconomic, subpar, supernova, underclass

USE APOSTROPHES

· To form possessive of a singular noun or a plural noun not ending in *s*, add an apostrophe and an *s*.
Richard's thesis.   *children's* toys.

· To form possessive of a plural noun ending in *s*, add only an apostrophe.
motorists' maps

PUNCTUATION

· To form the possessive of a singular proper noun, add an apostrophe and an *s*.

Poe's short stories   **Williams's** latest movie

· To form the possessive of a plural proper noun, add only an apostrophe.

the **Jeffersons'** family home

· To form the possessive of nouns in series when the possession is shared, add an apostrophe and an *s* after the last noun.

Jane, Bill, and **Rose's** office

· To form the possessive of nouns in series when possession is separate, add an apostrophe and an s after each noun.

Jane's, Bill's, and **Rose's** offices

USE PERIODS

· To end a declarative or imperative sentence.

The Russians are coming.   *Face left.*

QUESTION MARKS

· To end interrogative sentences.

How is Bill feeling today?

· Inside closing quotation marks if the quotation is a question.

The teacher asked, *"What time did you finish the test?"*

· Outside closing quotation marks if the whole sentence is a question.

Why is everyone saying, "I know the answer"?

· Inside closing quotation marks when it replaces a comma or period.

"Where has everyone gone?" Mary asked.

SPELLING

PREFERRED AND CONSISTENT SPELLING

Use the latest edition of a good collegiate dictionary as your reference. The **American Psychological Association** accepts the **Merriam-Webster Collegiate Dictionary** as its standard spelling reference. Use the first spelling listed.

WORD-WRAP

Do not hyphenate words at the ends of lines. Use the word-wrap feature of your word processor. If a word does not fit at the end of a line leave the line short.

GRAMMAR AND USAGE

AGREEMENT OF SUBJECT AND VERB

A verb must agree in number and person with its subject even when phrases or clauses separate them.

Wrong:

This *car,* in addition to hundreds of others, *were* selected for export.

Correct:

This *car,* in addition to hundreds of others, *was* selected for export.

***WITH INDEFINITE PRONOUNS:** **either, neither, everybody, everyone, somebody,** and **everything** are singular and must agree with a singular verb.*

Wrong:

Everyone of the cars *are* on the list.

Correct:

Everyone of the cars *is* on the list.

***WITH COLLECTIVE NOUNS:** **class, committee, assembly, series,** may be either singular or plural depending on whether the action is on a single group or the individuals within it.*

Action on whole group:

The (whole) *class was selected* to play.

Action on individuals:

The *class* (members) *are* divided on the issue.

WITH PAIRED COORDINATING CONJUNCTIONS: Neither...nor and ***either...or***

When one noun is singular and one is plural, the verb agrees with the closer noun.

Wrong:
```
Neither his brothers nor Dick were present.
```
Correct:
```
Neither his brothers nor Dick was present.
```

AGREEMENT OF PRONOUNS AND ANTECEDENTS
A pronoun must agree with its antecedent.

WITH INDEFINITE ANTECEDENT PRONOUNS: either, neither, everybody, everyone, somebody, **and** ***everything*** **are singular and must be followed by singular pronouns.**

Wrong:
```
Everyone is looking for their books.
```
Correct:
```
Everyone is looking for his or her books.
```

WITH PAIRED COORDINATING CONJUNCTIONS: Neither...nor **and** ***either...or.*** **When one noun is singular and one is plural, the pronoun agrees with the closer noun.**

Wrong:
```
Neither his brothers nor Dick has their
books.
```
Correct:
```
Neither his brothers nor Dick has his books.
```

PRONOUNS: *WHO* AND *WHOM*
Who **is a subject of a verb and** *whom* **is an object of a verb or preposition. An easy way to see if the use is correct is to turn the construction around and substitute** *he* **or** *him.* **If** *he* **fits,** *who* **is correct. If** *him* **fits, whom is correct. Remember,** *whom* **and** *him* **both end in the letter** *m.*

Wrong:
```
Who do you work for?   (You work for he.)
```
Correct:
```
Whom do you work for?   (You work for him.)
```

RELATIVE PRONOUNS: *THAT* AND *WHICH*

That introduces an element which, if omitted, would change the meaning of the sentence.

> Trees **that are green year round** are called evergreen.

Which introduces an element which, if omitted, would not change the meaning of the sentence.

> Trees, **which are among nature's gifts**, inspire me to write.

SUBORDINATE CONJUNCTIONS: *BECAUSE* AND *SINCE*

Because is used to indicate a causal relationship.

> The device failed **because** preparation was poor.

Since is used to indicate time.

> **Since** the beginning of the test period, several students have reported feeling ill.

MISPLACED MODIFIERS

Be certain modifiers are placed correctly to be sure the meaning is clear.

Bad:

> The dog is for sale. He eats anything and **loves children.**

(Does he love eating children?)

Better:

> The dog is for sale. He **loves children** and eats anything.

Bad:

> **Working hard on the term paper, the teacher** told John he was doing well.   **(Who is working on the term paper?)**

Better:

> **Working hard on the term paper, John** was praised by his teacher.

GRAMMAR-USAGE

2-7

PARALLEL CONSTRUCTION

Be sure that all sentence elements which express parallel ideas are in the same form.

AFTER COORDINATING CONJUNCTIONS: and, but, or, and nor

Wrong:

The author concluded that gross **sales** had improved but the individual **stores** had not. **(comparing sales with stores)**

Correct:

The author concluded that gross **sales** had improved, but that individual store's **sales** had not.

WITH PAIRED COORDINATING CONJUNCTIONS: not only...but also, both...and, either...or, neither...nor, between...and

• **both ...and**

Wrong:

The courses advertised were **both** *interesting* and *of great difficulty.* **(present participle and prepositional phrase)**

Correct:

The courses advertised were **both** *of great interest* and *of great difficulty.* **(two prepostional phrases)**

• **not only...but also**

Wrong:

Members were **not only** *upset* with the vote, **but also** *they resented the officious manner* of the president. **(single adjective and independent clause)**

Correct:

Members were **not only** *upset* with the vote, **but also** *resentful* of the officious manner of the president. **(adjective and adjective)**

• **neither...nor and either...or**

Wrong:

Neither the *girls' scores* on the first trial **nor** the *scores of the boys* were correctly recorded. **(adjective modifying noun and prepositional phrase modifying noun)**

Correct:
Neither the *girls' scores* on the first trial **nor** the *boys' scores* were correctly recorded. **(adjective modifying noun and adjective modifying noun)**

· **Between...and**
> **Wrong:**
> The difference **between** the *ideas* of the world leaders **and** the local *politicians* is apparent. **(noun-ideas and noun-people)**
> **Correct:**
> The difference **between** the *ideas* of the world leaders **and** the *opinions* of the local politicians is apparent. **(noun-ideas and noun-opinions)**

· **Among elements in series**
> **Wrong:**
> They were asked *to return* early, *to clean* the site, and *that the group begin* the new work. **(two infinitive phrases and a subordinate clause)**
> **Correct:**
> They were asked *to return* early, *to clean* the site, and *to begin* work. **(three infinitive phrases)**

IMPROVING WRITING STYLE

VARYING SENTENCE OPENINGS

Avoid the immature style of sentences which always begin with a subject. Use some of the openings suggested below.
> **Single Word Modifiers:** adjectives or adverbs set off with a comma.
> **Phrases:** groups of words with neither a subject or predicate.
> **Clauses:** groups of words with subjects and predicates.
> > Subordinate clauses cannot stand alone as a sentence, but usually modify the independent clause.

SINGLE WORD MODIFIERS

Nervously, he walked to the podium.
Disgusted, Mary turned and walked away.

PREPOSITIONAL PHRASES

After the test, the subjects left.
With brown stains, the coats looked awful.
Down with taxes was the party's war cry.

PRESENT PARTICIPIAL PHRASES

Walking quickly, the group left.
Standing alone, the painting was beautiful.
Writing a term paper is not easy.

PAST PARTICIPIAL PHRASES

Exhausted by his efforts, he died.
Overjoyed with the news, Bob jumped up.
Betrayed by his men, the general resigned.

INFINTIVE PHRASES

To avoid arrest, the immigrants fled.
To make a deal, he will do anything.
To live free is a blessing.

SUBORDINATE CLAUSES

Because the law called for the death penalty, no other verdict was possible.

If the results differ, the careful researcher should examine the procedures.

Although he believed her story, the reporter continued to investigate.

When he attempted to fly the latest model, he lost control of the airplane.

Whether or not he succeeded is not the question.

VARYING SENTENCE LENGTH

Short sentences are excellent to add emphasis or to describe very complicated ideas, but do not overuse them. Add variety by using simple, compound, complex or compound-complex sentences.

SIMPLE SENTENCE: One independent clause
> The Republican convention takes place in August.

COMPOUND SENTENCE: Two independent clauses
> The project took two months, but the result was worth the wait.

COMPLEX SENTENCE: An independent and a subordinate clause
> When he took the witness stand, we knew he would commit perjury.

COMPOUND-COMPLEX SENTENCE: Two or more independent and one or more dependent clauses
> He expressed no opinion, and when the others disagreed, he adjourned the meeting.

AVOIDING PASSIVE VOICE

In the passive voice of verbs, the subject of the sentence is the receiver of the action. The use of passive voice gives a dull tone to your writing.

> The message was sent by his friends.

Switch to the active voice in which the subject of the sentence does the action.
> His friends sent the message.

MAINTAINING VERB TENSE CONSISTENCY

In general, try to maintain the same tense throughout the paper. However, in formal research writing some shifts are acceptable.

PAST TENSE: Action that took place in the past.
> Richardson *described*

PRESENT PERFECT TENSE: Action that started in the past and continues to present.
> Richardson *has shown*

These tenses are appropriate for review of research literature or discussion of the work of others.

TRANSITIONS

PAST TENSE
skill development *improved*
Appropriate for describing the results of experiments in APA papers

PRESENT TENSE: Action which takes place in the present.
The results of the investigation *indicate*
Appropriate for discussing results and presenting conclusions in APA papers.

PAST PERFECT TENSE: Action which began in the past and was ended in the past.
The students *had completed* all their work before we arrived.

FUTURE PERFECT TENSE - Action which will begin in the future and end at a specific time in the future.
All of the students *will have received* their grades by this time tomorrow.

WRITING SMOOTH TRANSITIONS

Strive for smoothness in the joining of ideas. Use good transitional words between sentences, and effective transitional sentences between paragraphs or major thoughts. Following are examples of linking words which may be used alone or to introduce transitional phrases, clauses, or sentences.

Contrast:	but, however, although, nevertheless, on the other hand, conversely
Addition:	furthermore, moreover, similarly, for example, along with
Cause-Effect:	as a result, consequently, therefore, because
Time:	next, then, after, since, during, first, afterward, immediately
Location:	among, behind, across, near, beside, down, between, inside
Summary:	consequently, therefore, finally, thus

AVOIDING WORDINESS

Brief, sharp, incisive writing is preferred to long-winded words and phrases which do not enhance understanding. Think of the main idea and state it using a powerful verb. Do not use a thesaurus to find a longer word to impress your teacher or audience.

> **Bad:**
> Researchers have been exploring the outer reaches of space in an effort to discover life forms on other planets, but have not been successful at this time.
>
> **Better:**
> Researchers have not found life on other planets.

AVOIDING JARGON

Writers often overuse technical vocabularies which are obstacles to clear understanding.

> **Bad:**
> Computer programmers are exploring the infrastructure of cyberspace and prioritizing goals for exploiting business use of the Internet.
>
> **Better:**
> Computer programmers are working to find profitable business uses of the Internet.

AVOIDING SLANG AND COLLOQUIAL LANGUAGE

Avoid slang and colloquial expressions. Use formal English. Do not use contractions.

> **Bad:**
> He didn't lose his cool and just blew him off.
>
> **Better:**
> He kept his composure and ignored him.

WORDINESS-JARGON

ELIMINATING BIAS

Careful writers avoid language which may improperly generalize about gender, ethnic groups, socioeconomic class, sexual orientation, religion, and age.

Improper	Proper
mankind, man	people, humankind
stewardess, police woman	flight attendant, police officer
foreman, mailman	supervisor, postal worker
housewife	homemaker
disabled	man with an orthopedic disability.
he will use the machine	he or she will use the machine
his difficulties	his or her difficulties
White, Non-White, Oriental	White, African American, Asian
males, females	men, women, (for high school age or younger - boys, girls)
male nurse	nurse
chairman	chair or chairperson
depressives	people who are depressed

ELIMINATING BIAS

Basic PC Instructions

The following pages will help if you are unfamiliar with basic computer operations. On the other hand, if you are familiar with Windows and computers, you can skip this chapter and go directly to the word processing program you are using.

WHAT IS WINDOWS?

Windows is an operating system that runs various software applications such as word processors, spread sheets, business programs, desktop publishing programs, and others in your computer. Windows is called a graphical user interface (GUI) because it uses pictures to help you communicate with the machine.

WINDOWS RELEASES

Beginning with 3.0, Windows has been improved and upgraded several times with Windows 95, 98, 2000, and ME. The latest release, Windows 2000, is actually an upgrade of Microsoft NT which has been used with networked computers. ME is designed for personal users.

All of the Windows programs operate similarly with improvements offered with each new release. Beginning with Windows 95 users found the following enhancements:

* **Easier Program Starting**
* **Running Programs Simultaneously**
* **Switching Between Open Programs**
* **Easier Handling of Files and Folders**
* **Faster Operation**
* **Recycle Bin for Deleted Files**

THE WINDOWS DESKTOP

When your computer starts, the Windows desktop appears. "Shortcuts," icons of applications, are on the desktop and are used for opening word processing or other applications. All it takes is a double click on one of the icons. You can add your additional shortcuts later..

Typical Windows Desktop

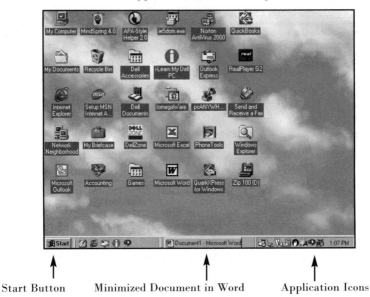

Start Button   Minimized Document in Word   Application Icons

Just above is an illustration of a typical Windows desktop which you might see on starting your computer.

The Start button is at the left side of the Taskbar which lies along the bottom of the desktop. The Taskbar is always visible. To the right of the Start button you will find small icons for applications. If you minimize an open application such as Microsoft Word, it will appear as a button on the Taskbar. Clicking on the button will re-open the application. In the illustration above the Microsoft Word application has been minimized and it appears on the Taskbar.

CONTROL THE COMPUTER WITH MOUSE OR KEYBOARD
USING THE MOUSE

The mouse controls the I-beam or pointer. Slide the mouse around on a flat surface moving it in the direction you want to move the I-beam or pointer. If it hangs up or if you seem to run out of room, lift the mouse and set it down in a new spot and try again.

Several terms will be used for the mouse in this book.

Pointer:	The pointer may change its appearance. It may be an arrow, an I-beam, or other shape, depending on what the computer is doing.
Click:	Move the mouse pointer to the place you want, press the left button once and release it.
Double Click:	Click the left button twice in rapid succession.
Drag:	Move the pointer to a place, hold down the button, move the pointer to a new place, and release.
Select:	Drag the pointer across text and release. Text will be highlighted.
Right Click	Click the right side of the divided mouse. A drop-down list will appear with contents depending on the location of the pointer.

USING THE KEYBOARD

All the words in the Menu Bar have a single letter underlined. Pressing Alt + the underlined letter will cause a drop down list to appear. Pressing the underlined letter in the words in the drop-down lists will open other drop-down lists or cause dialog boxes to appear. Sometimes you must press additional keys such as the Ctrl key to carry out the command. In some cases the final command has to be made by moving and clicking the mouse. Pressing Enter when a button in a dialog box is highlighted will carry out the command.

Using the keyboard to navigate around the screen.

Direction Keys:	The up, down, left, and right arrow keys are located on the lower right side of the keyboard. They can move the I-Beam in those directions.

MOUSE & KEYBOARD

Delete Key: Deletes characters selected as well as any characters to the right of the cursor.

Backspace Key: Deletes characters selected as well as characters to the left of the cursor.

End Key: Moves the cursor to the end of a line.

Home Key: Moves the cursor to the beginning of a line.

Ctrl Key: Executes commands when pressed with other keys. The keys are noted in the Menu command drop down lists.

Alt Key: Executes commands when pressed with other keys.

Function Keys: Located along the top of the keyboard, they execute special commands in various software application programs.

STARTING PROGRAMS WITH DESKTOP ICONS

Look back at the illustration on page 3-2.

1. Move the pointer over the icon on the desktop of the application you want to open.
2. Double click the icon of the application. The application will open.

or

1. Right click the icon. A pop-up menu will appear.
2. Click on Open or press O on the keyboard. The application will open.

STARTING PROGRAMS FROM THE START BUTTON

1. Click the Start Button. A pop-up menu will appear.
2. Slide the pointer up to Programs. Another pop-up menu will appear alongside the first.
3. Without lifting the mouse, slide the pointer to the name of the application you want to open and click on it. The application will open.

See the illustration on the next page.

OPENING AN APPLICATION FROM THE START BUTTON

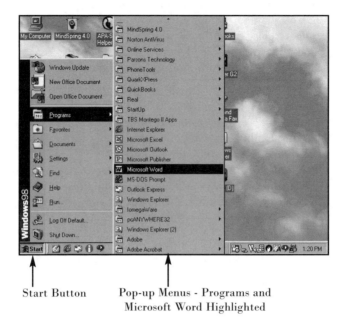

Start Button   Pop-up Menus - Programs and
Microsoft Word Highlighted

TYPICAL WINDOWS APPLICATION WINDOW

Minimize - Maximize - Close Buttons

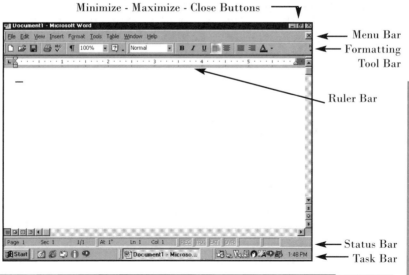

Menu Bar
Formatting
Tool Bar

Ruler Bar

Status Bar
Task Bar

QUITTING A WINDOWS 95 APPLICATION

There are several ways to quit an application.

1. Click on the **Control Menu Icon** in the upper left corner and choose **Close** from the drop-down list.
2. Choose **Exit** in the **File Menu.**
3. Click on the **Close Button in the upper right corner.**

EXITING WINDOWS

1. Be sure to close all programs before shutting down **Windows.** There should be no tasks or applications on the **Taskbar.**
2. Click **Start.** The **Start Menu** will open.
3. Click **Shutdown.** The **Shutdown Windows Dialog Box** will open with the **Shut down option button** highlighted.
4. Click **Yes or OK.** Windows will shut down.
5. Turn off the computer.

COMMON ELEMENTS IN ALL WINDOWS RELEASES

MENUS

Commands in **Windows** and all **Windows** applications are grouped in **Menus** which appear just below the **Title Bar** of an open window. These generally include the commands **File, Edit, View**, and **Help.** In addition, the commands **Insert, Format, Tools, Table, and Window** usually appear in application programs.

TYPICAL MENU BAR

File   Edit   View   Insert   Format   Tools   Table   Window   Help

TO OPEN A MENU WITH THE MOUSE

1. Click on the command you want to open. A **drop down list** of additional commands will appear.
2. Move the **arrow pointer** down the list until you reach the command you want. Click on the command.

TO OPEN A MENU WITH THE KEYBOARD

1. Press **Alt+the underlined letter** of the **Menu Name.** For example, to open the **File Menu,** press **Alt+F.** A drop down list of additional commands will appear.
2. Press the **underlined letter** of the command you want.

MENU CONVENTIONS

1. **Command dimmed:** Means this command is not available. For example, if you try to select **Copy** from the **Edit Menu** without selecting the text to be copied, the command will be dimmed. However, if you select text in the document, the command becomes active.

2. **Ellipsis (...):** Means that a **Dialog Box** will open if you select the command because the program needs more information from you before it can carry out its work.

3. **Check Mark:** Means that the command is already active. A **bullet** is used instead of a check mark in **Windows 95.**

4. **Short Cut Keys:** Means press these keystrokes to carry out the command without having to open the **Menu** or choose a command from the drop down list. For example, pressing **Ctrl+C** will copy selected text.

5. **A Right Arrow:** Means that a second drop down menu will appear with additional commands when you click on the command.

MENU BAR

TYPICAL MENU DROP DOWN LIST

TOOLBARS

Toolbars are groups of **icon buttons** or **text buttons** which represent tasks. You can add or delete specific toolbars by checking each in the **View Menu**. The **Standard** and **Formatting Toolbars** are usually selected to be displayed. However, several more specialized toolbars are available to be displayed depending on the special projects your are working on. For example, **Word 2000** has **Drawing, Picture,** and **Web Toolbars** in addition to others.

TOOLBARS

TYPICAL FORMATTING TOOLBAR

Toolbar: Contains several buttons which are short cuts for tasks such as **File, Print, Spell Check, Save, Cut, Copy, Paste** In addition, it will contain drop-down lists and buttons for quick formatting of text with **Font, Font Size, Bold, Italic,Underlining, Justification, etc.**

RULER BAR

Ruler Bar: Displays a ruler which can be used to set **Tabs, Indents,** and **Margins** quickly.

STATUS BAR

| Page 1 | Sec 1 | 1/1 | At 1" | Ln 1 | Col 1 | REC | TRK | EXT | OVR |

Status Bar: A bar at the bottom of the screen which tells you the page number, line number, column, as well as any information based on the **Menu** item selected.

DIALOG BOXES

A dialog box appears when the computer needs to have a "dialog" with you to understand the choices you want to make in **Menu Commands.** There are several basic options or controls you manipulate in dialog boxes.

TOOLBARS

Option Buttons: A series of circles alongside options. A dot will appear when you click in the circle you want.

Check Boxes: A series of squares alongside options. A check mark or X will appear when you click in the square you want.

Text Boxes: A rectangular box in which you type information. If the box is empty when you move to it, the cursor will be flashing and you can begin typing. If selected text already appears and it is correct, press **Tab** to move to the next option. If it is incorrect, simply type the correct information and it will replace what was there.

List Boxes: A box containing a list of options from which you can choose. If the list is too long, scroll bars are added. Click the option you want to select.

Drop-Down List Boxes: A list box containing a single item with a down arrow alongside. Click the **arrow** and an **option list** will drop down. Click the option you want to select.

Command Buttons: Rectangular buttons which carry out commands such as **OK, Cancel,** or **Help.**

Spin Boxes: A box for changing measurements by clicking up or down arrows or by typing in a number.

Tabs: Used to change pages in a dialog box

WINDOWS 2000 DIALOG BOX

Option Buttons

Text Box

Spin Boxes

Drop-down List Boxes

Command Buttons

BASIC WORD PROCESSING

SELECTING TEXT

1. Move the **I-beam** to the right of the word or words to be selected.
2. Drag the **I-beam** across the word or words.
3. To select several lines or paragraphs, drag the **I-beam** toward the bottom of the page.

COPYING TEXT

1. Select text.
2. Choose **Copy** from the **Edit Menu.**
3. Move the cursor to the spot where you want the text to go.
4. Choose **Paste** from the **Edit Menu.**

WORD PROCESSING

MOVING TEXT

1. Select text.
2. Choose **Cut** from the **Edit Menu.**
3. Move the cursor to the spot where you want the text to go.
4. Choose **Paste** from the **Edit Menu.**

DELETING TEXT

1. Select text.
2. Press the **Delete Key**. If you accidentally delete text, immediately choose **Undo** from the **Edit Menu.**
3. Single characters can be deleted by pressing the **Backspace Key** after a character or the **Delete Key** before a character.

Part Two

Using the *MLA Handbook* to Write Your Paper

Word Processing Applications

Part Two

Using the *MLA Handbook* to Write Your Paper

Word Processing Applications

Author-Page Citation

MLA Handbook for Writers of Research Papers, 5th Ed., 1999

The **Modern Language Association** is a scholarly organization which traces its roots to 1883. One of its aims has been to standardize and codify practices for researchers and writers. **MLA** style has its widest use among the humanities, but other disciplines have also adopted it.

The latest edition of the *MLA Handbook* contains simplified rules for documenting sources using citations placed in parentheses directly in the text. There is no longer a need for difficult footnoting or endnoting.

The *MLA Handbook* also includes documentation guidelines for new electronic sources such as CD-ROMs, electronic journals and e-mail.

PARENTHETICAL AUTHOR-PAGE CITATION

The author's name and the specific page number(s) where the material is located in the work are placed in parenthesis in the text. When the author's name appears in the text only the page number(s) need to be placed in the parenthesis. A little practice may be necessary to insert the references and keep the writing fluent. Author-page citation samples are on pages 4-2 through 4-4.

Every source cited in the text must be documented in a Works Cited list at the end of the paper. It is important that references be cited accurately. Works cited samples, single spaced to save space, are on pages 4-5 through 4-14.

PUNCTUATION OF AUTHOR-PAGE CITATIONS

It is preferable to place the parenthetical reference at the end of the sentence. End the sentence without punctuation. Leave one space and add the parenthetical reference followed by the appropriate punctuation mark. Exception: When long quotations are set off from the text, leave one space after the end punctuation and add the parenthetical reference without any punctuation.

PARENTHETICAL AUTHOR-PAGE CITATION

BOOK - SINGLE AUTHOR
Insert the last name(s) of the author(s) and page number(s) in the parentheses.

> This concept has been reported earlier (Jones 148).

or

If author's name appears in the text, insert only the page number(s) in the parenthesis.

> Jones reported this concept (148).

BOOK - MULTIPLE AUTHORS
Insert all authors' last names and the page number(s) in the parenthesis.

> An opposing idea has been explored (Brown, Smith, and Rogers 179-81).

or

If authors' names appear in the text, insert only the page number(s) in the parenthesis.

> Brown, Smith, and Rogers explored an opposing idea (179-81).

MULTIPLE WORKS BY THE SAME AUTHOR(S)
If two or more works by the same author(s) will be cited, insert author(s) name(s) followed by a comma, the title, if short, or a short version, and the page number(s) in the parenthesis.

> Most humans experience depression, often for reasons unknown to them (Rogers, <u>Psychology</u> 171-73).

or

If author(s) name(s) and title appear in the text, insert only the page number(s) in the parenthesis.

> In <u>Psychology and Modern Man,</u> Rogers explains that most humans experience depression, often for reasons unknown to them (171-73).

PARENTHETICAL AUTHOR-PAGE CITATION

or
If two or more works by same author will be cited and author's name appears in text, insert the title and page number in the parentheses.

Rogers explains that most humans experience depression, often for reasons unknown to them (Psychology and Modern Man 171-173).

WHOLE WORK
Author's name and title of whole work may appear in text without parentheses.

Shakespeare's Hamlet has been called his most enigmatic tragedy.

MULTI-VOLUME WORK
Insert author's name and volume number followed by a colon, space and page number(s) in parentheses.

Economic policy should provide for maintenance of full employment (Johnson 2: 273).

or
If author's name and volume appear in the text, place only the page number(s) in parentheses.

In volume 2, Johnson suggests that economic policy should provide for maintenance of full employment (273).

or
If the whole volume is cited without reference to pages, insert the author's name and abbreviation for volume in the parentheses.

Economic policy should provide for maintenance of full employment (Johnson, vol. 2).

CORPORATE OR GOVERNMENT PUBLICATIONS
Insert corporate author in text and place page number(s) in parentheses.

In 1984 the United States Department of Defense issued a report denying activity in Paraguay (31).

or
Insert corporate author and page number(s) in parentheses.

A recent report denies any United States activity in Paraguay (United States Department of Defense 31).

PARENTHETICAL AUTHOR-PAGE CITATION

MAGAZINE OR JOURNAL ARTICLES
Use same techniques as for books

NOVELS
Insert the page number followed by a semicolon and the chapter number preceded by the abbreviation for the part or chapter.

> The opening words of <u>Moby Dick</u>, "Call me Ishmael," quickly identify the narrator (1; ch.1).

PLAYS
Insert division: act, scene, canto, book, or part and line(s) separated by periods in the parentheses but omit page numbers. In general, use arabic numerals rather than roman unless otherwise directed.

> The queen finds relief in believing her son, Hamlet mad (3.4.105).

POETRY
Cite by division and line: canto, book, or part separated by periods in the parenthesis (similar to plays), but omit page numbers. If only lines are cited, spell out the word, line or lines, and type the number(s).

> Shelley's "Ozymandias" ironically describes the ephemeral nature of fame and power in the statement, "Look on my works, ye Mighty, and despair! / Nothing beside remains (lines 10-13).

WORK LISTED BY TITLE
Insert title or abbreviation and page number(s) in parentheses

> The <u>New Yorker</u> reprinted a story on country dining ("Country Inns and Byways" 213).

or
Insert title of whole unsigned work in parentheses

> The spectrum is visible when white light is sent through a prism ("Color and Light").

ONLINE SOURCES
If no page numbers are given, omit page numbers and use appropriate sample from above.

> Braking reaction time varied widely (Rabine).

MLA WORKS CITED SAMPLES

WORKS CITED

A bibliography called **Works Cited,** printed on a separate page at the end of the paper, provides complete publication information for all of the sources cited in your paper. The citations in the text must lead the reader to the source in the **Works Cited** bibliography.

Start the list on a new page. Center the words, Works Cited, in upper and lower case on the top line. Double space and type the first entry. Type the first line flush left and indent following lines, if any, one half inch. Double space between and within entries.

Samples shown below are single spaced to save space.

BOOKS

BOOK - NO NAMED AUTHOR
Handbook of Pre-Columbian Art.   New York:
    Johnson, 1988.

BOOK - ONE AUTHOR
Gershman, Herbert S.   The Surrealist Revolution
    in France.   Ann Arbor: U of Michigan P,
    1994.

BOOK - MULTIPLE AUTHORS
Raffer, Bernard C., Richard Friedman, and Robert
    A. Baron.   New York in Crisis.   New York:
    Harper, 1986.

BOOK - SAME AUTHOR(S) - USE 3 HYPHENS AFTER FIRST ENTRY
---.   A Study of Life.   New York: Norton, 1993.

BOOK - EDITED
Melville, Herman.   Moby Dick.   Ed.   J.P. Small.
    Boston: Houghton, 1973.

BOOK - TRANSLATION
Maurois, Andre.   Lelia.   Trans.   Gerard Hopkins.
    New York: Harper, 1954.

BOOK - CORPORATE AUTHOR
National Policy Association.   Welfare Reform.
    New York: McGraw, 1992.

MULTIVOLUME WORK - CITING ONE VOLUME ONLY
Smith, Richard K.   A History of Religion in the
    United States.   Vol. 3.   Chicago: U of
    Chicago, 1993.

MLA WORKS CITED SAMPLES

MULTIVOLUME WORK - CITING MORE THAN ONE VOLUME
Smith, Richard K. <u>A History of Religion in the
    United States</u>. 4 vols. Chicago: U of
    Chicago, 1993.

GOVERNMENT PUBLICATION
United States. Dept. of Labor. <u>Labor Relations
    in the Steel Industry</u>. Washington: GPO,
    1994.

DISSERTATION - UNPUBLISHED
Samson, Robert. "The Influence of Economic
    Deprivation on Academic Achievement." Diss.
    New York U, 1985.

DISSERTATION - PUBLISHED BY UNIVERSITY MICROFILMS
Garon, Lois. <u>Socialist Ideas in the Works of
    Emile Zola</u>. Diss. Brown U, 1992. Ann
    Arbor: UMI, 1993. 921437.

POEMS, ESSAYS, SHORT STORIES, PLAYS IN ANTHOLOGIES
Poe, Edgar Allan. "The Raven." <u>Great American
    Poetry</u>. Ed. Richard Johnson. New York:
    McGraw, 1978. 38-40.

ARTICLE IN REFERENCE BOOK - UNSIGNED
"DNA." <u>Encylopedia Americana</u>. 1994 ed.

ARTICLE IN REFERENCE BOOK - SIGNED
Smith, Richard. "Color and Light." <u>Encyclopedia
    Britannica</u>. 1994 ed.

PERIODICALS

NEWSPAPER ARTICLE - SIGNED
May, Clifford. "Religious Frictions Heat Up in
    Rwanda." <u>New York Times</u> 12 Aug. 1994, late
    ed.: A1.

MAGAZINE ARTICLE - UNSIGNED
"Making of a Candidate for President." <u>Time</u> 20
    July 1984: 40-42.

MAGAZINE ARTICLE - SIGNED
Kuhn, Susan. "A New Stock Play in Saving and
    Loans." <u>Fortune</u> 15 May 1995: 67-72.

MLA WORKS CITED SAMPLES

EDITORIAL - UNSIGNED
"China's Conscience." Editorial. <u>New York Times</u> 19 May 1995, late ed.: A22.

EDITORIAL - SIGNED
Brownhurst, Marshall S. "Rush to Judgement." Editorial. <u>Wall Street Journal</u> 5 June 1995: A15.

ABSTRACT IN ABSTRACTS JOURNAL
Frischman, Josephine K. "Analysis of Bias in Selecting Test Times." <u>Journal of Experimental Psychology</u> 98 (1992): 325-31. <u>Psychological Abstracts</u> 80 (1993): item 7321.

ARTICLE IN LOOSELEAF COLLECTION - SOCIAL ISSUES RESOURCES SERIES - SIRS
Cruver, Philip C. "Lighting the 21st Century." <u>Futurist</u> Mar. 1990: 29-34. <u>Energy</u>. Ed. Eleanor Goldstein. Vol. 4. Boca Raton: SIRS, 1991. Art. 84.

ARTICLE IN MICROFICHE COLLECTION - NEWSBANK
Chieper, Randy. "Welfare Reform Debates." <u>New York Times</u> 20 Apr. 1994, late ed.: A12. <u>Newsbank: Welfare and Social Problems</u> 17 (1994): fiche 2, grids A9-13.

REVIEW OF BOOK, FILM, OR PERFORMANCE INCLUDE AUTHORS, DIRECTORS, CONDUCTORS, PERFORMERS, OTHERS AS PERTINENT
Maslin, Janet. "New Challenges for the Caped Crusader." Rev. of <u>Batman Forever</u>, dir. Joel Schumacher. <u>New York Times</u> 16 June 1995, late ed.: C1.

ARTICLE - SIGNED IN JOURNAL WHICH USES ISSUE NUMBERS
Brogdan, Robert. "Religious Freedom and School Holidays." <u>Phi Delta Kappan</u> 68 (1984): 700-02.

ARTICLE - SIGNED IN JOURNAL WHICH PAGES ISSUES SEPARATELY
Jones, Mary. "Urban Poetry." <u>American Review</u> 13.2 (1987): 66-73.

MLA WORKS CITED SAMPLES

NON-PRINT SOURCES

TELEVISION OR RADIO PROGRAM
**Include if appropriate "Episode Title." <u>Program Title</u>. Series Title.
Actors. Directors. Producers. Network. Call Letters, City. Date.**

"Pollution in the Desert." Narr. Mike Wallace.
Prod. Jock Fenway. Dir. John Brett. <u>Sixty
Minutes</u>. CBS WCBS, New York. 6 Mar. 1994.

SOUND RECORDING
**Cite first whichever is emphasized: Composer. Performer. Conductor.
<u>Title</u>. Artists. Audiocasssette or LP if not a CD. Manufacturer, Date or
N.D. if unknown.**

Webber, Andrew Lloyd. <u>Phantom of the Opera</u>.
Perf. Michael Crawford, Sarah Brightman, and
Steve Barton. Audiocassette. EMI, 1987.

FILM
**Include <u>Title</u>. Director. Also, if pertinent, Writers. Performers.
Producers. Distributor, Year.**

<u>Raiders of the Lost Ark</u>. Dir. Steven Spielberg.
Paramount, 1982.

INTERVIEW - BROADCAST

Gramm, Phil. Interview with Charlie Rose.
<u>Charlie Rose</u>. WNET, New York. 6 May 1994.

INTERVIEW - PERSONAL

Kennedy, Robert. Personal Interview. 11 Jan.
1971.

ELECTRONIC PUBLICATIONS

The citation of print publications has long been standardized, but with the coming of electronic publishing, scholars have only begun to lay down the basic rules for citing this new material. Because electronic publications are not as permanent as bound paper volumes, more bibliographic information is required for these works. For example, if the work was originally in print, the print bibliographical data should be included.

The sample citations which follow conform to those recommended in the *MLA Style Manual and Guide to Scholarly Publishing*, 2nd ed. 1998 and the *MLA Handbook for Writers of Research Papers*, 5th ed. 1999.

MLA WORKS CITED SAMPLES

CD-ROM - DISKETTE - MAGNETIC TAPE

NON-PERIODICAL DOCUMENT ON CD-ROM, DISKETTE, OR MAGNETIC TAPE

Include Author (or if only editor or translator instead of author follow with a comma and abbreviation). Title. Editor or Translator (if relevant). Publication Medium. Edition or Version (if relevant). Place of Publication: Publisher, Electronic Publication Date.

Conrad, Joseph. Victory. CD-ROM. Cambridge, Eng.: Chadwyck-Healey, 1994.

Braunstein, Roger, ed. Hamlet. By William Shakespeare. CD-ROM. New York: Hastings, 1996.

United States. Dept. Of Commerce. "Railroad Tonnage Reports." 1993. National Trade Data Bank. Magnetic Tape. US Dept. of Commerce. Apr. 1994.

NON-PERIODICAL DOCUMENT ON CD-ROM, DISKETTE, OR MAGNETIC TAPE PREVIOUSLY IN PRINT

Author. Title. Print Publication Information. Publication Medium. Place of Publication: Publisher, Electronic Publication Date.

Hemingway. Complete Works of Hemingway. Ed. Richard Jomes. Columbus: Ohio UP, 1993. CD-ROM. New York: Gale, 1996.

PERIODICAL DOCUMENT ON CD-ROM, DISKETTE, OR MAGNETIC TAPE ALSO PUBLISHED IN PRINT

Author. "Title." Print Publication Information. Database Title (if available). Publication Medium. Vendor. Electronic Publication Date.

Barron, James. "New York Welfare Programs in Jeopardy." New York Times 8 May 1995, late ed.: C1. New York Times Ondisc. CD-ROM. UMI-Proquest. Nov. 1995.

TELEVISION OR RADIO PROGRAM ON CD-ROM, DISKETTE, OR MAGNETIC TAPE

Sills, Beverly. "Opera Today." Interview. Charlie Rose. PBS. 15 August 1995. Transcript. Broadcast News. CD-ROM. Primary Source Media. Jan. 1996. 19 screens.

MLA WORKS CITED SAMPLES

FILM OR FILM CLIP ON CD-ROM, DISKETTE, OR MAGNETIC TAPE
Binder, Mike, dir. <u>Crossing the Bridge</u>. 1995.
    CD-ROM. New York: Touchstone, 1997.

WORK OF ART ON CD-ROM
Van Gogh, Vincent. <u>Trees in the Asylum Garden</u>.
    1889. <u>Microsoft Art Gallery: The Collection</u>
    <u>of the National Gallery, London</u>. CD-ROM.
    Redmond: Microsoft, 1996.

ONLINE SOURCES

Because there is yet no agreed upon standard for what publication information should be included for electronic works and because electronic media often "disappear" or are modified, great care must be used in citing these works. The version you access may differ from the original so it is important to include the access date as well as the original date if available.

For material which appeared first in print, the dates of print and electronic publication as well as the access date should be provided. The Uniform Resource Locator (URL) is the best way to identify an online source. However, care should be used in transcribing URLs because of the possibility of error. If you need to divide a URL between two lines, do so only after a slash. Use no hyphen at the break. Enclose the URL in angle brackets.

ONLINE SCHOLARLY PROJECT

<u>Title</u>. Project Editor (if available). Electronic Publication Information including Version Number (if relevant). Date of Electronic Publication. Sponsoring Institution. Date of Access Electronic Address.

<u>Voice of the Shuttle: English Literature</u>
    <u>Restoration and Eighteenth Century</u>. Ed. Alan
    Liu. Apr. 1998. U of California, Santa
    Barbara. 20 June 1998 <http://
    humanitas.ucsb.edu/shuttle/eng-18th.html>.

POEM OR OTHER MATERIAL IN AN ONLINE SCHOLARLY PROJECT

Author's Name. "Title." <u>Project Title</u>. Project Editor (if available). Electronic Publication Information including Version Number (if relevant). Date of Electronic Publication. Sponsoring Institution. Date of Access Electronic Address.

Butler, Josephine E. "Native Races and the War."
    <u>Victorian Women Writers Project</u>. Ed. Perry
    Willet. 1998. Indiana U. 15 May 1998
    <http://www.indiana.edu/~letrs/vwwp/butler/
    native.html>.

MLA WORKS CITED SAMPLES

PROFESSIONAL OR PERSONAL SITE
Name of Site Creator (if given). <u>Site Title</u> (if there is one or the words Home Page not underlined. Institution or Organization (if associated with site). Access Date Electronic Address.

<u>Chartered Institute of Marketing Page</u>. 22 Jan. 1998 <http://www.cim.co.uk/>.

ONLINE BOOK
Author (if given). or Editor or Translator with appropriate abbreviation (ed., trans.), <u>Title</u>. Editor or Compiler or Translator (if relevant). Print Publication Information (if relevant). Access Date. Electronic Address.

Conrad, Joseph. <u>Heart of Darkness</u>. New York: Harper Brothers, 1910. 15 Jan. 1998 <http://sunsite.berkeley.edu/Literature/ Conrad/Heart of Darkness/01.html>.

Paine, Thomas. <u>The Rights of Man</u>. 1792. 12 Apr. 1998 <gopher://gopher.vt.edu:10010/02/ 129/4>.

ONLINE PERIODICALS
Author (if given). "Title." <u>Periodical Name</u>. Volume and or Issue Number (if given) Publication Date. Number of Pages or Paragraphs (if numbered). Access Date Electronic Address.

ONLINE NEWSPAPER
Bradley, Ann. "Educated Consumers." <u>Education Week on the Web</u>. 26 Mar. 1997. 4 Apr. 1998 <http://www.edweek.org/ew/vol-16/ 26consum.h16>.

ONLINE SCHOLARLY JOURNAL
Curley, Thomas. "Johnson and America." <u>The Age of Johnson</u> 6 (1994) 22 Apr. 1998 <http:// www.english.upenn.edu/~Jlynch/AJ/>.

Schneider, Joe. "A Cautionary Word About Charters." <u>The School Administrator</u> 54.7 (1997). 22 Jan. 1998 <http://www.aasa.org/ SchoolAdmin/aug9703.htm>.

MLA WORKS CITED SAMPLES

ONLINE SCHOLARLY JOURNAL

"Events in Congress: March 20-April 2, 1998."
     <u>Chronicle of Higher Education</u>. 20 Mar.
     1998. 15 Apr. 1998 <http://
     chronicle.merit.edu/.events/.ewash.html>.

ONLINE REVIEW (May be Untitled)

Brailsford, William. Rev. of <u>The Laurel and the
     Ivy: The Story of Charles Stewart Parnell
     and Irish Nationalism</u>, by Robert Kee.
     <u>Crisis Magazine</u> (1996). 12 June 1998 <http://
     www.eppc.org/library/articles/brailsford/
     brev_feb96.html>.

ONLINE MAGAZINE ARTICLE

Thompson, Dick. "Rendezvous for Old Rivals." <u>Time</u>
     27 Mar. 1995. 20 Apr. 1998 <http://www.
     pathfinder.com/time/magazine/archive/1995/
     950327/950327.space.html>.

Gobel, Dave. "Distance Learning - Educating in
     Cyberspace." <u>Online Magazine</u> 12 Apr. 1998.
     9 May 1998 <http://www.online-magazine.com/
     lgu.html>.

ONLINE EDITORIAL (May be Untitled)

"Small Schools as an Investment." Editorial. <u>New
     York Times on the Web</u> 1 May 1988. 20 May
     1998 <http://www.nytimes.com/yr/mo/day/
     editorial/01fri3.html>.

ONLINE ABSTRACT

Green, R.J. "Intelligent Robotic Systems: A
     Research Perspective." <u>Abstracts of MJCS</u>
     6.11 (1996): 11-12. Abstract. 13 May 1997
     <http://mjcs.fsktm.um.edu.my/MJCS/Volume_6/
     VOL_6_No1.1>.

ONLINE LETTER TO THE EDITOR (May be Untitled)

Harrison, Lawrence E. Letter. <u>New York Times on
     the Web</u> 4 May 1998. 18 June 1998 <http://
     www.nytimes.com/yr/mo/day/letters/
     lharri.html>.

MLA WORKS CITED SAMPLES

OTHER ELECTRONIC SOURCES

ONLINE TELEVISION OR RADIO PROGRAM
Baron-Faust, Rita. "Night Vision Loss." <u>Report on Medicine</u>. CBS Radio. WCBS, New York. 4 May 1998. Transcript. 10 June 1998 <http://newsradio88.com/medicine/history/may_1998/may_4.html>.

ONLINE MAP
"Maps of Liberia." Map. Geography and Map Division. Library of Congress. 15 Mar. 1998 <http://memory.loc.gov/ammem/gmdhtml/libhtml/libhome.html>.

ONLINE WORK OF ART
Wores, Theodore. <u>A Garden Shrine, Sugita</u>. Spanierman Gallery, New York. 12 June 1998 <http://spanierman.com/wores.htm>.

ONLINE CARTOON
Trudeau, G.B. "Doonesbury." Cartoon. <u>New York Times on the Web</u>. 5 May 1998. 6 Aug. 1998 <http://www2.uclick.com/client/nyt/db/>.

ONLINE POSTING
Author. "Title," (from subject line) Online posting. Date of Posting. Forum Name. Access Date List Address or E-mail Address of List Moderator
Glavac, Maria S. "Busy Educator's Guide." Online posting. 5 May 1988. NETTRAIN Digest. 26 May 1988 <listserv@listserv.acsu.buffalo.edu>.

ONLINE SOUND CLIP OR SOUND RECORDING
Pershing, John J. "From the Battlefields of France." 1918. <u>American Leaders Speak: Recordings from World War I and the 1920 Election</u>. 1996. <u>American Memory</u>. Lib. of Congress, Washington. 20 June 1998 <http://lcweb2.loc.gov/ammem/nfexper.html>.

MLA WORKS CITED SAMPLES

ONLINE POEM

Coleridge, Samuel T. "Kubla Khan." 1798. Jan.
    1998 <http://english-www.hss.cmu.edu/
    poetry/kubla-khan.html>.

ONLINE GOVERNMENT DOCUMENT

U. S. Dept. of State. Counter Terrorism
    Rewards Program. (1998). 21 Feb. 1998
    <www.heroes.net/pub/heroes/
    content2.html>.

FILE TRANSFER PROTOCOL (FTP)

"In the Courts." National Newsletter of the ACLU.
    Spring 1994. 14 Nov. 1997 <ftp://ftp.psi.
    net/aclu/newsletter/380courts>.

E-MAIL

**Include Name of Writer,"Message Title," (if any) found on the subject
line, description of the message including the recipient, date of message.**

Richardson, Robert. E-mail to the author. 14 July
    1997.

Casserly, James. "Aviation News." E-mail to
    Robert A. Baron. 27 Jun. 1998.

MLA QUOTATIONS

Prose

Quotations of four lines or less are not set off from the text but are placed within double quotation marks. Quotations may be placed at the beginning, middle, or end of sentences.

```
Thomas Paine, in his pamphlet, The Crisis,

wrote the stirring line, "These are the times

that try men's souls."
```

If the quotation ends the sentence and a parenthetical citation is required, omit the period in the sentence and place the period after the reference.

```
Thomas Paine, in his pamphlet, The Crisis,

wrote the stirring line, "These are the times

that try men's souls"  (14).
```

For longer quotations, use a comma or colon after the last word of text, double space and type the quotation with no quotation marks. Indent ten spaces or one inch from the left margin and double space quote. Parenthetical citations following longer quotations follow the punctuation at the end of the last sentence.

```
Writing to bolster the country after the

discouraging first days of the war, Paine

wrote:

      These are the times that try men's

      souls.  The summer soldier and the

      sunshine patriot will, in this crisis,

      shrink from the service of their

      country; but he that stands it now,

      deserves the love and thanks of man and

      woman. (18)
```

4-15

If two or more paragraphs are quoted one after another, indent the first line of each paragraph three more spaces or an additional quarter of an inch. If the first paragraph quoted does not begin a paragraph in the original, do not indent it.

Use double quotation marks for quotations within a long quotation.

Poetry

Poetry of three lines or less is placed in double quotation marks within the text. Separate lines of poetry which appear in a single line of text by a slash (/) with a space before and after the slash.

```
Robert Frost's short poem describing how

fate  plays a role in human lives, ends

with the lines, "Two roads diverged in a

wood, and I-- / I took the one less

traveled by, / And that has made all the

difference (11).
```

For longer poems, use same procedure as for prose. Lines which do not fit on one line should be continued on the next line and indented three spaces or an additional quarter of an inch. To improve appearance, it is OK to indent fewer than ten spaces or one inch if that will allow the longer lines to fit on one text line. Unusual spacing of poetry should be followed as closely as possible.

Drama

Use a comma or colon after the last word of text, double space and indent ten spaces or one inch from the left margin. Capitalize the character's name, punctuate with a period and type the quotation. Indent following lines by the same character three spaces or an additional one quarter inch. Begin following character's lines by indenting ten spaces or one inch. Parenthetical citations follow the punctuation at the end of the last quoted line.

```
The opening lines of Shakespeare's Hamlet

create a mood of foreboding with this
```

exchange between the guards:

> BERNARDO. Who's there?
>
> FRANCISCO. Nay, answer me. Stand
>
> and unfold yourself! (1.1.1-2)

Punctuation of Quotations

Periods and commas are placed inside quotation marks. Question marks and exclamation marks not originally in the quotation go outside the quotation marks. If a parenthetical reference ends a quoted line, place the period after the reference.

Quotation Within a Quotation

Use single quotation marks to set off a quotation within a quotation.

Ellipsis

When omitting words, phrases or sentences from quoted material, enclose three spaced periods within square brackets. Do not space after the first bracket or after the last period.

Ellipsis in the Middle of a Quoted Sentence

Leave a space before the first bracket and after the last bracket.

> Describing the differences between the views
> of Western and non-Western nations about ethnic
> cleansing, Michael Wines states, "But to many
> other nations, the Kosovo atrocities [...] were
> just the broken eggs of yet another national
> omelet, and the West was a self-righteous, ever-
> more meddlesome cook."

Ellipsis at the End of a Quoted Sentence
Leave a space before the first bracket, place the closing period after the last bracket with no space and end with a quotation mark

Describing the differences between the views of Western and non-Western nations of ethnic cleansing, Michael Wines writes, "But to many other nations, the Kosovo atrocities that Germany equated with its own past and President Clinton labeled 'vicious' and 'terrifying' were just the broken eggs of yet another national omelet [...]."

MLA NUMBERS

In general use arabic numerals for all numbers not spelled out, except for the occasional use of roman numerals.

♦ **Spell numbers of one or two words.**
three   one thousand   five million

♦ **Use numerals for numbers of more than two words.**
3.56   2,456   1,489, 602

♦ **Use numerals for numbers which precede units of measurement.**
24 volts   121.5 megahertz, 6 centimeters

♦ **Use numerals for numbers in comparisons of data.**
The July temperature ranged from 67 to 90.

♦ **Use numerals with abbreviations, addresses, dates, and page numbers.**
12 lbs. $10.00   316 5th Avenue   page 3
April 21, 1929

♦ **Use a combination of numerals and words for large numbers.**
14.7 billion dollars

♦ **Use capital roman numerals in outlines and after names of individuals**
Henry VIII   Richard III   Topic III

♦ **Use lowercase roman numerals for pages of a book which are numbered in roman numerals.**
page iv

SAMPLE MLA FIRST TEXT PAGE (TITLE PAGE)

½″

Quarles   1

3 spaces

Roger P. Quarles

Double
space
Professor Onklaw

Sociology 112

9 September 1995

Center title

→ Workfare Programs in Three States

Double space

President Clinton pledged an "end to welfare as we know it"

as part of the 1992 election campaign. However, the

administration has been unable to get the Congress to act on the

suggested reforms and, as a result, the states have proposed a

wide range of experimental initiatives (Kellam 795). Several are

1″ → based on the concept of workfare, a popular idea with both ← 1″ →

Republicans and Democrats.

When Congress passed the Jobs Opportunities and Basic Skills

Program (JOBS) in 1988, it gave states matching funds to develop

programs. Wisconsin, Delaware, and California are among the

states which have begun workfare programs (796).   ← Author-page citation

However, the picture is not altogether sanguine. Some critics of

the workfare concept including Gilbert claim that workfare will

increade welfare costs and simultaneously increase the numbers of

homeless persons (795). There are arguments that despite the

faults of the old AFDC program fifty percent of recipients are

off welfare within two years (Gilbert 47). Others state that a

lack of funds for job training and child care will make workfare

programs impossible to maintain (Kaus 23).

Wisconsin's workfare program, often cited as a model, has

not worked well for the clients or the employers its critics say.

The goal, simple as it sounds, to reduce dependence on welfare by

putting people back on their feet, is obviously not as easy as

1″

SAMPLE MLA TEXT PAGE
WITH AUTHOR-PAGE CITATION

1"

Quarles   2

it seems. Still there are some successes and the lessons learned
from the experimentation of the states has been invaluable. The
problem is a major one for America as seen by the statistics.
Ten years ago fewer than four million families received welfare.
Currently, five million families with about 14 million people
receive benefits under the welfare system (Kellam 795).

Delaware's Department of Health and Social Services
implemented its First Step Employment and Training Program in
1986, even before Federal legislation under the JOBS program.
Under the current system, applicants eligible for Aid to Families
with Dependent Children must enroll in an educational program,
which frequently leads to a general equivalency diploma (GED).
Candidates may be referred to the Delaware Technical and
Community College for eight weeks of training in "life skills."

1"

With intitiative, some qualify for degrees from the college with
support from regular monthly benefit payments, child care and
Medicaid (Kaus 23).

Author-page citation

About 1.1 billion dollars in federal aid was available under
the JOBS program to states capable of putting up matching funds.
The federal government provided 1.8 million dollars to Delaware
and the state matched with $978,558. The state now operates 12
multi-service centers that serve as one stop facilities for
individuals and families seeking federal aid (Kellam 796).

As late as August, 1994 President Clinton and Senator Dole
presented different visions of welfare reform to state governors.
Clinton took administrative action to approve state programs
which put welfare recipients to work and which denied increases
in food stamps to those who will not take jobs (795).

1"

SAMPLE MLA TABLE

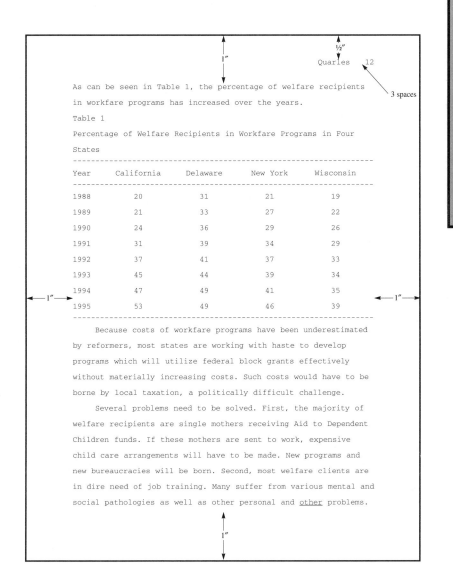

As can be seen in Table 1, the percentage of welfare recipients
in workfare programs has increased over the years.

Table 1

Percentage of Welfare Recipients in Workfare Programs in Four
States

Year	California	Delaware	New York	Wisconsin
1988	20	31	21	19
1989	21	33	27	22
1990	24	36	29	26
1991	31	39	34	29
1992	37	41	37	33
1993	45	44	39	34
1994	47	49	41	35
1995	53	49	46	39

Because costs of workfare programs have been underestimated
by reformers, most states are working with haste to develop
programs which will utilize federal block grants effectively
without materially increasing costs. Such costs would have to be
borne by local taxation, a politically difficult challenge.

Several problems need to be solved. First, the majority of
welfare recipients are single mothers receiving Aid to Dependent
Children funds. If these mothers are sent to work, expensive
child care arrangements will have to be made. New programs and
new bureaucracies will be born. Second, most welfare clients are
in dire need of job training. Many suffer from various mental and
social pathologies as well as other personal and other problems.

Quarles 12

3 spaces

½″

1″

1″

1″

1″

MLA TABLE

MLA HANDBOOK

SAMPLE MLA WORKS CITED PAGE

Works Cited

Bernstein, Phillip R., Charles D. Delanson, and Paul Connelson.

"Attitudinal Changes in Mothers Engaged in Job Training."

Journal of Applied Psychology 78 (1993): 452-457.

Carlson, Roberta J. _The Dream and the Dilemma: Welfare in_

America. New York: Macmillan, 1994.

Conniff, Ruth. "Cutting the Lifeline: The Real Welfare Fraud."

The Progressive Feb. 1992: 25-28

Cowan, Noah. "The Big Lie About Workfare." _Utne Reader_ May-

June 1992: 28-29.

Gilbert, Neil. "Why the New Workfare Won't Work." _Commentary_

May 1994: 47.

Kaus, Mickey. "Tough Enough: A Promising Start on Welfare

Reform." _The New Republic_ 25 Apr. 1994: 22-23.

Kellam, Susan. "Welfare Experiments: Are States Leading the Way

Toward National Reform?" _Congressional Quarterly Researcher_

16 Sept.1994: 795-796.

Robinson, Karl, and Bernard R. Politcheck. _The Politics of_

Welfare Reform. New York: McGraw Hill, 1994.

Schwartz, Miriam. "The Role of the Mother in AFDC Families."

Consulting Psychology Journal: Practice and Research 45.4

(1993): 27-29.

United States. Dept. of Health and Human Services. _Survey of_

Jobs Training Programs. Washington: GPO, 1992.

"Workfare Debate Heats Up in Legislatures." _Washington Post_ 21

Aug. 1993: A3.

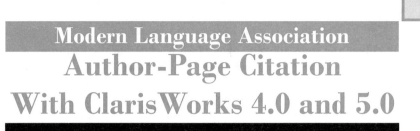

Modern Language Association
Author-Page Citation
With ClarisWorks 4.0 and 5.0

OPENING CLARISWORKS THE FIRST TIME

Windows 3. 1

1. At the **DOS** prompt, **C:\>**, type **win** and press **Enter.** The **Program Manager Window** will appear with several icons.
2. Double click on the ClarisWorks Icon. The **ClarisWorks Window** will appear.
3. Double click on **Word Processing.** A **Blank Document Page** will appear with the cursor flashing at the left margin.

Windows 95, 98, and 2000.

1. Click the **Start Button.** Choose **Programs,** the **ClarisWorks Folder,** and **ClarisWorks 4. 0** or **5.0** icon. The **ClarisWorks New Document Dialog Box** will appear with **Word Processing** and **Create New Document** highlighted.
2. Click on **OK.** A **ClarisWorks Word Processing Document Window** similar to the one below will appear.

CLARISWORKS WORD PROCESSING DOCUMENT WINDOW

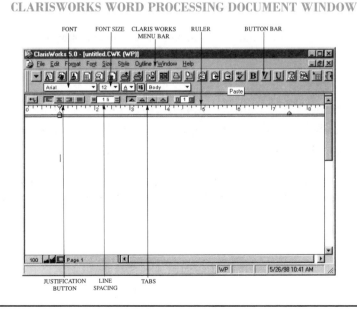

OPENING YOUR DOCUMENT LATER

1. Follow the steps above to open **ClarisWorks** from the **Program Manager Window** in **Windows 3. 1** or the **Start Button** in **Windows 95.**
2. Choose **Open** from the **File Menu** or click on the **Open File Button** in the **Default Button Bar.** The **Open Dialog Box** will appear.

ClarisWorks 4.0

3. Look for your document in the **File Name: list box**. If not there, click the down arrow next to the list box to scroll through the list until you see your document.

ClarisWorks 5.0

3. Look for your document in the list. If not there, click on the down arrow in the Look in Box to show the various drives. Click the drive or directory in which your document was saved.
4. Click on your document to highlight it and click **OK.** Your document will appear with its name in the **Title Bar.**

MARGINS

The setting for **MLA** papers is one inch on top, bottom, and sides which is the default setting for **ClarisWorks.** You can change the margins if required by your instructor, but do not right justify or hyphenate words.

1. Choose **Document** in the **Format Menu.** The **Document Dialog Box** will open.
2. Type the modified margins in inches in each of the **Margins Boxes.**
3. Click on **OK.**

LINE SPACING

MLA papers are double spaced throughout. The default setting for **ClarisWorks** is single spacing. Change the setting before you begin typing.

1. Click the **Increase Spacing Button** with two horizontal bars in the **Button Bar.** It is between the **Tabs** and **Justification Buttons.** The setting in the window will shift to **2 li.**

FONT

Font is the term used to describe the shape of the type used in typing. The **MLA** suggests using a standard typeface in

10 or 12 point size similar to that found in typewriters. **Courier** and **Times Roman** are good examples. Although **ClarisWorks** enables you to change the font, the size, and a whole range of styles such as bold, condensed, and shadow, select one simple typeface and keep it in the plain text style.

`This is 12 point Courier font.`

1. Choose **Courier** in the **Font Menu or** in the **Pop-up Menu** in the **Button Bar.**
2. Choose **12 Point** in the **Size Menu or** in the **Pop-up Menu** in the **Button Bar.**

ITALICS AND UNDERLINING

Prior to the invention of computers and word processing programs, writers used underlining to designate words which were to be italicized by the printer. Many colleges and universities still require such underlining and frown on the use of italics in formal papers. You should discuss this matter with your instructor if you wish to use italics.

Foreign words and the titles of books, magazines, and newspapers are underlined to indicate italics.

1. Select the text you want to underline or italicize.
2. Choose **Underline** in the **Style Menu** or the **Pop-up Menu**, or click the **U Button** in the **Button Bars.**
3. Choose **Italic** in the **Style Menu** or the **Pop-up Menu**, or click the *I* **Button** in the **Button Bars.**

CENTERING AND JUSTIFYING

Justification describes how words are placed on the page: flush left, flush right, or centered. **ClarisWorks** allows you to spread the words on each line across the page so the right margin is straight or right justified. Although **MLA** papers should not be justified, you will need to center or move some text at times.

1. Select the text you want to center or move.
2. Find the four **Justification Buttons** with several horizontal lines symbolizing lines of text under or over the ruler in the **Button Bar.**
3. Click on the **Center Justification Button** to center text.
4. Click on the appropriate **Justification Button** to move text left or right.

INDENTION

MLA papers are indented one half inch.

1. To change indentation in a paragraph, place the **cursor** in the paragraph.
2. Drag the **first line, left,** and **right indent markers** to the proper positions on the ruler. In **ClarisWorks 4.0** the **first line indent marker** is a short horizontal line, the **left margin marker** is a right pointing triangle, and the **right margin marker** is a left pointing triangle. In **ClarisWorks 5.0** the **first line indent marker** is a down pointing arrow, the **left margin marker** is an up pointing arrow, and the **right margin marker** is an up pointing arrow.
3. To indent the first line of a paragraph, drag the **first line indent marker** one half inch to the right of the **left margin marker.**
4. To change the left or right margins of the paragraph, drag the **left** and **right margin markers** to the appropriate position on the ruler.

PAGINATION

Beginning with the first page, **MLA** papers carry a right justified heading one half inch from the top of the page with your last name in upper and lower case followed by the page number in arabic numerals. **See sample pages on pages 4-19 through 4-22.**

1. Choose **Insert Header** from the **Format Menu.** A blinking cursor will appear at the left margin in a **Header box.**
2. Choose **Insert Page #** from the **Edit Menu.** Click **OK**.
3. The cursor will appear just to the right of the number 1 at the left margin. Press the **Left Arrow Key** to move the cursor to left of number 1.
4. Press the **Space Bar** three times to move the number 1 three spaces to the right.
5. Press the **Left Arrow Key** three times to move the cursor to the left margin.

6. Type your last name. The cursor will be at the last letter of your name.
7. Press the **Left Arrow Key** to move the cursor to the beginning of your name.
8. Click the **Right Justification Button** in the **Button Bar.** Your name and page number 1 will shift to the right margin.
9. Click at the left margin of the first line of the text space under the header box to move the cursor there.

TITLE PAGE

MLA papers do not have a formal title page. **Your name, instructor's name, course number,** and **date** are grouped at the upper left corner of the first page. **See sample Title Page on page 4-19.**

1. Move the cursor to the top line of the first page.
2. Type in upper and lower case, **your full name,** first name first, on the top line, the **instructor's name** on the second line, the **course number** on the third line, and the **date** on the fourth line, double spaced at the left margin.
3. Double space and center the **title** in upper and lower case.
4. Double space and begin your paper.

AUTHOR-PAGE CITATIONS

MLA papers use a simple system of citing sources by stating the author's name and page number(s) of the work in parentheses. Citations are placed directly in the text. No special keystrokes are necessary. The citations lead readers to the alphabetical list of sources in the **Works Cited** list at the end of the paper. **Follow the explanation and examples of parenthetical citations on pages 4-2 through 4-4. See the sample Text Page with author-page citations on page 4-20.**

1. Citations are placed directly in the text. No special keystrokes are necessary.

WORKS CITED LIST

The **Works Cited** list is printed at the end of the paper and presents the full bibliographic information for every source cited in the body of your paper. Do not include sources you may have consulted, but did not use. It is a good idea to prepare the **Works Cited** list before you actually start the paper so you will know how to cite the references in the text. **See the sample formats for Works Cited entries on pages 4-5 through 4-14 and the sample Works Cited page on page 4-22.**

1. Move the cursor to the end of the last line of text. Press **Enter** to place the cursor on a new blank line.
2. Choose **Insert Break** from the **Format Menu.** The cursor will move to a new page.
3. Center the words, **Works Cited,** in upper and lower case on the top line. Double space.
4. Type entries in alphabetical order using the appropriate format for the type of reference you are citing. The first line of each entry begins at the left margin with following lines double spaced and indented a half inch.
5. Double space within and between entries.

TABLES

Tables should be used sparingly. Use them only when data will be better presented in tabular form. Avoid confusing the reader by breaking up text with too many tables. Do not duplicate information in the text which appears in a table. A table should supplement material in the text, but it should also be understandable alone.

Tables are assigned arabic numerals and brief titles and are located as close as possible to their mention in the text. Every column must have a short heading. The data in the left column usually describes the major independent variable.

Use horizontal rules only and use vertical spacing to make the table easily readable. Double space within tables.

See the sample Table on page 4-21.

Although **ClarisWorks** has a program to set up tables automatically, **MLA** tables are very simple with no vertical rules and only a few dashed horizontal rules. The easiest and quickest way to prepare tables is to use tabs.

1. Move the cursor to the place in the text where the table will be inserted. Leave three blank lines.
2. Type the words, **Table 1**, flush left without a period.
3. Double space and type the **title** flush left in upper and lower case. Extra lines of title are centered and double spaced.
4. Double space and type a **line of hyphens** across the page.
5. You must now set up the rows and columns which make up the table. Each column must have a header and these should be spaced evenly across the top of the table. The first column of the table is at the left margin. The last column should be near the right margin.

Setting Tabs for Headers

6. Type the **first header** flush with the left margin. Capitalize the first letters of major words in each heading.
7. Find the **four Tab Triangles** on the **Button Bar.** One is **shaded** on the **left**, one on the **bottom**, one on the **right**, and one on the **top**. The one shaded on the left aligns columns on the left side of the tab, the one shaded on the bottom centers columns on the tab, the one shaded on the right aligns columns on the right side of the tab, and the one shaded at the top aligns columns of numbers along a decimal point.
8. Drag the **Center Triangle Tab Icon** to the approximate location on the ruler where the second header should be. Follow the same procedure for the remaining header locations.
9. Press the **Tab Key** and type the second header under its **Tab Icon.** Press the **Tab Key** again and type the third header. Continue the procedure until all headers are typed.
10. Select any header and drag its **Triangle Tab Icon** left or right. The header will move with the icon to a new location. Use this method to adjust the locations of the headers until they are properly spaced.
11. Double space and type a line of hyphens under the headers.

Entering Data

12. Double space and enter data under each header by pressing tab to reach the next column. When you type the numbers to enter data, they will be centered under the **Tab Icons.** Be sure to align decimal points using the **Decimal Point Tab Icon.**
13. Double space and type a line of hyphens across the page.
14. Double space and continue typing your document.

SPELL CHECK

1. Choose **Check Document Spelling** in the **Writing Tools Submenu** of the **Edit Menu** or click the **ABC Button** on the **Default Button Bar.** The **Spelling Dialog Box** will appear over the document window with misspelled words highlighted.
2. Click on one of the word options offered to correct it.
3. Click on **Replace** to replace the misspelled word with the correct one. Click on **Learn** if the word is a special use word not in the **Spell Check** dictionary.
4. Continue the process until the entire document been checked.

PRINTING

1. If you are using your computer in a lab and there are several printers, choose **Print Setup** from the **File Menu.** The **Print Setup Dialog Box** will appear. Choose the correct printer for your job.
2. Choose **Print** from the **File Menu** or click the **Print Button** on the **Default Button Bar.** The **Print Dialog Box** will appear. Change any other print settings as required. Click **Print** or **OK.**

SAVING

1. The first time you save a document choose **Save As** from the **File Menu.** The **Save As Dialog Box** will appear.
2. The **Cursor** will be blinking in the **File Name: Box.** Type the name of your document with no more than 8 characters in **ClarisWorks 3 & 4.**

ClarisWorks 3 and 4

3. **Drive C** is selected in the **Drives: Box** or you may change it.
4. Choose a **Directory** where you want to save your document in the **Directories Scroll List. Clworks** is usual or change it. Click **OK.**

ClarisWorks 5

3. The name of the folder in which you document will be saved will be in the **Save in: Box.**
4. Click on **Save.**
5. To avoid disaster, click on the **Save Button** in the **Standard Tool Bar** every ten minutes. **ClarisWorks** will save your work to the hard drive and directory you selected in the **Save As Dialog Box.**
6. It is a good idea to save your document on another disk just in case the hard drive crashes or some other glitch which computers are known for develops. Choose **Save As** from the **File Menu.** The **Save As Dialog Box** will appear.
7. Insert a **floppy disk** in the **A: Drive.** Use the **down arrow** in the **Drives Scroll List or the Save in: Box** until the **A: Drive** appears.
8. Click **Save** or **OK.** Your document will be saved on the floppy disk.

Modern Language Association

Author-Page Citation
With WordPerfect 6-7-8-9

OPENING WORDPERFECT THE FIRST TIME

Windows 3. 1

1. At the **DOS** prompt, **C:\>** type **win** and press **Enter.** The **Program Manager Window** will appear with several icons.
2. Double click on the **WPWin group icon** in the **Program Manager Window.** The **group icon window** will open.
3. Double click on the **WPWin 6 icon.**
4. A blank document window will appear similar to the one shown below with a **Menu Bar, Title Bar, Toolbar,** and **Power Bar.**
5. The cursor or insertion point will be flashing at the left margin.
6. You are ready to begin typing your paper.

Windows 95, 98, and 2000.

1. Click the **Start Button.** Choose **Programs** and double click on the **WPWin 7, WPWin 8, and WPWin 9.**

WORDPERFECT DOCUMENT PAGE WINDOW

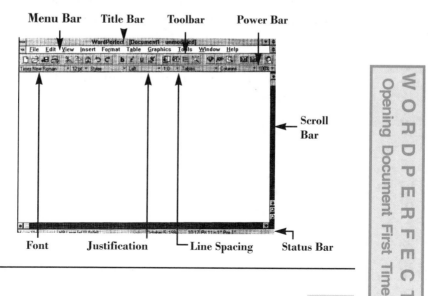

OPENING YOUR DOCUMENT LATER

1. Follow the steps above to open **WordPerfect.**
2. Choose **Open** from the **File Menu** or click the **Open Button** in the **Toolbar.** It is the second button on the left and contains a picture of a file folder being opened. An **Open File Dialog Box** will appear.
3. Look for the name of your document in the **Filename: list box** in **WordPerfect 6, File List** in **WordPerfect 7,** or **Name text box** in **WordPerfect 8 and 9.** If you do not see the document, click the down arrow next to the list box to scroll through the list until you see your document name.
4. Click on your document to highlight it and click **OK** in **WordPerfect 6** or double click on your document in **WordPerfect 7, 8,** and **9.** Your document will appear with the name in the **Title Bar.**

MARGINS

The setting for **MLA** papers is one inch on top, bottom, and sides which is the default setting for **WordPerfect.** You must change the top margin to print the header containing the page number at the right location. You can change the margins if required by your instructor, but do not right justify or hyphenate words.

1. Choose **Margins** in the **Format Menu.** The **Margins Dialog Box** will open.
2. Change the **Top Margin** to **.5".** .
3. Make any other changes necessary.
4. Click on **OK.**

LINE SPACING

MLA papers are double spaced throughout. The default setting for **WordPerfect** is single spacing. Change the setting before you begin typing.

1. Choose **Line** and **Spacing** from the **Format Menu.** A **Dialog Box** will appear.
2. Type **2** and click **OK.**

or

1. Click the **Line Spacing Button** in the **Toolbar in Word Perfect 7** or **Property Bar** in **WordPerfect 8** and **9** and click on **2.**

FONT

Font is the term used to describe the shape of the type used in typing. The **MLA** suggests using a standard typeface in 10 or 12 point size similar to that found in typewriters. **Courier** and **Times Roman** are good examples. Although **WordPerfect** enables you to change the font, the size, and a whole range of styles such as bold, condensed, and shadow, select one simple typeface and keep it in the plain text style.

This is 12 point Courier font.

1. Choose **Font** from the **Format Menu.** The **Font Dialog Box** will appear.
2. Click the up or down arrows to scroll through the **Font Face: scroll list** until you locate **Courier** or similar font.
3. Click the **up** or **down arrows** to scroll through the **Font Size scroll list** until you reach **12.**
4. Be sure to click on **Regular** in the **Font Style drop down list.**
5. Click on **OK.**

or

1. Click on the **Font** and **Size Buttons** in the **Power Bar** or **Toolbar.** Drop down lists will appear.
2. Click on **Courier** and **12.**

ITALICS AND UNDERLINING

Prior to the invention of computers and word processing programs, writers used underlining to designate words which were to be italicized by the printer. Many colleges and universities still require such underlining and frown on the use of italics in formal papers. You should discuss this matter with your instructor if you wish to use italics.

Foreign words and the titles of books, magazines, and newspapers are underlined to indicate italics.

1. Select the text you want to underline or italicize.
2. Choose **Font** from the **Format Menu**. The **Font Dialog Box** will appear.
3. Click **Underline** or **Italic** in the **Appearance Box**.
4. Click **OK**.

or

1. Select the text you want to underline or italicize.
2. Click on the *I* or <u>U</u> **Button** in the **Toolbar** or **Property Bar** in **WordPerfect 8** and **9.**

CENTERING AND JUSTIFYING

Justification describes how words are placed on the page: flush left, flush right, or centered. **WordPerfect** allows you to spread the words on each line across the page so the right margin is straight or right justified. Although **MLA** papers should not be justified, you will need to center or move some text at times.

1. Select the text you want to center or move.
2. Click on the **Justification Button** in the **Toolbar** or **Property Bar** in **WordPerfect 8** and **9** and drag down to **Left, Center,** or **Right** as needed.

INDENTION

MLA papers are indented one half inch. The **WordPerfect** default setting is one half inch, but you may want to change indents for quotations or other purposes.

1. Select the paragraph you want to indent.
2. Choose **Paragraph** in the **Format Menu.** The **Paragraph Format Dialog Box** will appear.
3. Change the **First Line Indent** by clicking on the up or down arrows.
4. Change the **Left** and **Right Margins** as required in the **Paragraph Adjustments Box.**
5. Click **OK.**

PAGINATION

Beginning with the first page, **MLA** papers carry a right justified heading one half inch from the top of the page with your last name in upper and lower case followed by the page number in arabic numerals. **See sample pages on pages 4-19 through 4-22.**

WordPerfect 6 and 7

1. Be sure the cursor is on the first page of your paper.
2. Choose **Header/Footer** in the **Format Menu.** A **Header/Footer Dialog Box** will appear.
3. Choose **Header A** and **Create** in the **Headers/Footers Dialog Box.** A new window will open with the **name of your document** and **Header A** in the **Title Bar.** A **Feature Bar** with several buttons will be at the top of the window. The cursor will be flashing at the left margin.
4. Type your **last name** and press the **Space Bar** three times to leave three spaces after your name.
5. Click on the **Number Button** in the **Features Bar.** The page number 1 will appear three spaces after your name.
6. Click on the **Justification Button** in the **Toolbar** and drag down to **Right.** The header with your name and page number will shift to the right margin.
7. Click on **Close.**

WordPerfect 8 and WordPerfect 9

1. Be sure the cursor is on the first page of your document.
2. Choose **Header-Footer** from the **Insert Menu.** A **Header-Footer Dialog Box** will appear.
3. Choose **Header A** and **Create** in the **Header-Footer Dialog Box.** The cursor will move to the **Header area** of the page. The words, **Header A**, will appear at the top of the screen next to your document name. Several buttons will be added to the **Property Bar.**
4. Type your **last name** and press the **Space Bar** three times to leave three spaces after your name.
5. Click on the **Number Button** in the **Property Bar.** It is the button with a #1 in a box.
6. Click on the **Justification Button** in the **Property Bar** and drag down to **Right**. The header with your name and page number will shift to the right margin.
7. Click on **Close.**

TITLE PAGE

MLA papers do not have a formal title page. **Your name, instructor's name, course number,** and **date** are grouped at the upper left corner of the first page. **See sample Title Page on page 4-19.**

1. Move the cursor to the top line of the first page.
2. Type in upper and lower case, **your full name,** first name first, on the top line, the **instructor's name** on the second line, the **course number** on the third line, and the **date** on the fourth line, double spaced at the left margin.
3. Double space and center the **title** in upper and lower case.
4. Double space and begin your paper.

AUTHOR-PAGE CITATIONS

MLA papers use a simple system of citing sources by stating the author's name and page number(s) of the work in parentheses. Citations are placed directly in the text. No special keystrokes are necessary. The citations lead readers to the alphabetical list of sources in the **Works Cited** list at the end of the paper. **Follow the explanation and examples of parenthetical citations on pages 4-2 through 4-4. See the sample Text Page with author-page citations on page 4-20.**

1. Citations are placed directly in the text. No special keystrokes are necessary.

WORKS CITED LIST

The **Works Cited** list is printed at the end of the paper and presents the full bibliographic information for every source cited in the body of your paper. Do not include sources you may have consulted, but did not use. It is a good idea to prepare the **Works Cited** list before you actually start the paper so you will know how to cite the references in the text. **See the sample formats for Works Cited entries on pages 4-5 through 4-14 and the sample Works Cited page on page 4-22.**

1. Move the cursor to the end of the last line of text. Press **Enter** to place the cursor on a new blank line.
2. Press **Ctrl + Enter.** A gray and black line will appear. The cursor will move to a new page.
3. Center the words, **Works Cited**, in upper and lower case on the top line. Double space.
4. Type entries in alphabetical order using the appropriate format for the type of reference you are citing. The first line of each entry begins at the left margin with following lines double spaced and indented a half inch. Double space between entries.

TABLES

Tables should be used sparingly. Use them only when data will be better presented in tabular form. Avoid confusing the reader by breaking up text with too many tables. Do not duplicate information in the text which appears in a table. A table should supplement material in the text, but it should also be understandable alone.

Tables are assigned arabic numerals and brief titles and are located as close as possible to their mention in the text. Every column must have a short heading. The data in the left column usually describes the major independent variable.

Use horizontal rules only and use vertical spacing to make the table easily readable. Double space within tables. **See the sample Table on page 4-21.**

Although **WordPerfect** has a program to set up tables automatically, **MLA** tables are very simple with no vertical rules and only a few dashed horizontal rules. The easiest and quickest way to prepare tables is to use tabs.

1. Move the cursor to the place in the text where the table will be inserted. Leave three blank lines.
2. Type the words, **Table 1**, flush left without a period.
3. Double space and type the **title** flush left in upper and lower case. Extra lines of title are centered and double spaced.
4. Double space and type a **line of hyphens** across the page.
5. You must now set up the rows and columns which make up the table. Each column must have a header and these should be spaced evenly across the top of the table. The first column of the table is at the left margin. The last column should be near the right margin.

Setting Tabs For Headers

6. Type the **first header** flush with the left margin. Capitalize the first letters of major words in each heading.
7. Choose **Ruler Bar** from the **View Menu**. The **Ruler** will appear with **Left Tab Stops** every half inch.
8. Place the cursor arrow in the bottom of the **Ruler** and click the **Right Mouse Button**. Drag down to **Clear All Tabs.** All the tab stops will disappear.
9. Click the cursor arrow in the bottom of the **Ruler.** Drag down to **Center.** This will change the **Left Tab Stops** to **Center Tab Stops** so all characters will be centered on the **Tab Stop.**
10. Place the cursor arrow in the bottom of the **Ruler** where you think the second header should be and click. A **Center Tab Stop** will be placed at the spot on the ruler.
11. Follow the same procedure for the remaining headers.

12. Type the headers moving the cursor with the **Tab Key**. If the spacing doesn't look right, select a header you would like to move, click on its **Tab Stop** and drag it left or right until the spacing looks correct. The headers will move with the **Tab Stops** as you drag them.

13. Double space and type a line of hyphens under the headers.

Entering Data

14. Double space and enter data moving the cursor with the **Tab Key**. If you want to enter decimal data, place the cursor arrow in the ruler, click the **Right Mouse Button**, and drag down to **Decimal**. Drag the **Center Tab Stop** off the **Ruler** and replace it with the **Decimal Tab Stop**. Decimal data entered will be aligned on the decimal points.

15. Double space after entering data and type a line of hyphens across the page.

Resetting Default Tab Settings

16. Double space.

17. To reset the **Default Tab Settings,** choose **Line** and **Tab Set** in the **Format Menu**. The **Tab Set Dialog Box** will appear. Click **Left** in the **Type Box, .500** in the **Position Box,** click on **Repeat Every .500,** and click **OK.**

18. Continue typing text.

SPELL CHECK

1. Move the cursor to the beginning of your paper.

2. Choose **Spell Check** from the **Tools Menu** or click the **Spell Check Button** in the **Toolbar**. It is on the right with an **Open Book icon**. The **Spell Checker** or **Writing Tools Dialog Box** will appear.

3. Click on options in the **Dialog Box** and be sure to choose all of the **Options** you want **Spell Checker** to do.

4. Click on **Start** if you have not selected **Auto Start** in **Options.**

5. **Spell Checker** will display the first misspelled word in the **Not Found: Box** and suggest a replacement word in the **Replace With: Box.** If the word is correct, click on **Replace.**

6. Other words will be suggested in the **Suggestions: List Box** in **WordPerfect 6** or in the **Replacements List Box** in **WordPerfect 7, 8,** and **9.** Click on the **correct word** and **Replace.**

7. If your paper contains a word which is not in the dictionary, but which is correct, click on **Add** to add the word to the dictionary.

8. **WordPerfect 6** has a **Quick Correct** feature which is called **Spell as You Go** in **WordPerfect 7, 8,** and **9.**

9. To start **QuickCorrect** in WordPerfect **6**, choose **Quick Correct** in the **Tools Menu.** The **QuickCorrect Dialog Box** will appear. Click in the **Replace Words as You Type box.** If you misspell a word such as "the" for "the," WordPerfect will type it correctly.

10. To start **Spell as You Go** in **WordPerfect 7, 8**, and **9**. choose **Proofread** and **Spell as You Go** from the **Tools Menu.** Misspelled words will be spelled correctly.

11. Misspelled words which are not in the dictionary will be marked with a **red underline. Right clicking** on the word will generate a drop down list of possible replacement words. Click on the **correct word** or click on **Skip in Document** if you want to ignore the misspelling or **Add** to add the word to the dictionary.

PRINTING

1. Choose **Print** from the **File Menu.**
2. Click on the selection you want to print in the **Print Selection Box** in **WordPerfect 6** or the **Print Box** in **WordPerfect 7, 8 and 9.** In most cases, you will select **Full Document.**
3. Click on the number of copies and click **Print.**

SAVING

WordPerfect 6 - WordPerfect 7 - WordPerfect 8 - WordPerfect 9

1. The first time you save your document choose **Save As** from the **File Menu.** The **Save As Dialog Box** will appear.
2. Type a file name for your document using no more than 8 characters without spaces in the **File Name Box.** WordPerfect 7, 8, and 9 allow you to use a name with up to 255 characters. The document will be saved to the hard drive, usually C:. Click on **OK.**
3. After you have named your document, choose **Save** from the **File Menu,** click on the **Save Button** in the **Toolbar,** or press **Ctrl+S** on the **Keyboard** every few minutes to avoid disaster.
4. It is a good idea to save your document to a floppy disk at the end of each session. Insert a formatted floppy in the A: drive.
5. Choose **Save As** from the **File Menu.**
6. Scroll down to the **A: drive** with the **Drives: Scroll Button.** Click on **OK.**

Modern Language Association
Author-Page Citation
Microsoft Word 6-7-97-2000

OPENING MICROSOFT WORD FIRST TIME

Windows 3. 1

1. At the **DOS** prompt, **C:\>**, type **win** and press **Enter**. The **Program Manager Window** will appear with several icons.
2. Look for either the **Microsoft Office icon** or the **Microsoft Word icon** If you see the **Microsoft Word icon**, double click on it. If you see the **Microsoft Office icon** first, double click on it and then double click on the **Microsoft Word icon**.
3. A blank **Microsoft Word Document Window** will appear similar to the one shown below with a **Menu Bar, Standard Toolbar, Formatting Toolbar, and** a **Ruler** under the **Menu Bar.**
4. The cursor will be flashing at the left margin.
5. You are ready to begin typing your paper.

Windows 95, 98, 2000

1. Click on the **Start Button** in the left corner of the **Taslbar.** Point to **Programs.** Click on **Microsoft Word.** A blank **Word Document Window** similar to the one below will appear.

MICROSOFT WORD DOCUMENT WINDOW

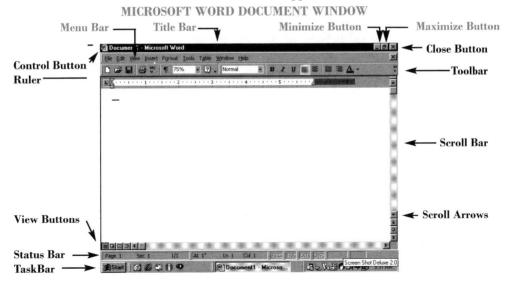

Menu Bar — Title Bar — Minimize Button — Maximize Button — Close Button — Control Button — Toolbar — Ruler — Scroll Bar — Scroll Arrows — View Buttons — Status Bar — TaskBar

7-1

OPENING YOUR DOCUMENT LATER

1. Follow the steps above to open **Microsoft Word** from the **Program Manager Window** in **3. 1** or the **Start Button** in **95, 98, and 2000.**
2. Choose **Open** from the **File Menu** or click the **Open Button** on the **Standard Toolbar.** It is the second button on the left and contains a picture of a file folder being opened. The **Open Dialog Box** will appear.
3. Look for the name of your document in the **File Name: list box** in **Word 6.** If you do not see the document, click the down arrow next to the list box to scroll through the list until you see your document name. Look in the **Look in: list box** in **Word 7** and **Word 97, 98, and 2000.** If you do not see your document, click on the **Up One Level Button** until you reach the folder you want to open.
4. Double click on your document. Your document will appear with the name in the **Title Bar.**

MARGINS

The setting for **MLA** papers is one inch on top, bottom, and sides. You can change the margins if required by your instructor, but do not right justify or hyphenate words.

1. Choose **Page Setup** in the **File Menu.** The **Page Setup Dialog Box** will appear.
2. Click on the **Margins Tab** and type **1"** in each of the **Top, Bottom, Left, and Right boxes.**
3. Be sure the setting in the **From Edge** area is **0.5"** since this is the distance between the **Header**, which will appear with page numbers on every page, and the top edge of the page.
4. Click on **OK.**

LINE SPACING

MLA papers are double spaced throughout. The default setting for **Microsoft Word** is single spacing. Change the setting before you begin typing.

1. Place the insertion point at the first line of your paper.
2. Choose **Paragraph** in the **Format Menu.** The **Paragraph Dialog Box** will open.
3. Choose **Double** from the **Line Spacing At: drop down list.**
4. Click **OK.**

FONT

Font is the term used to describe the shape of the type used in typing. The **MLA** suggests using a standard typeface in 10 or 12 point size similar to that found in typewriters. **Courier** and **Times Roman** are good examples. Although **Microsoft Word** enables you to change the font, the size, and a whole range of styles such as bold, condensed, and shadow, select one simple typeface and keep it in the plain text style.

This is 12 point Courier font.

1. Click on the **Font** and **Size Buttons** in the **Formatting Toolbar.** Drop down lists will appear.
2. Click on **Courier** and **12.**

or

1. Choose **Font** from the **Format Menu.** The **Font Dialog Box** will appear.
2. Use the **up** and **down arrows** to scroll through the list of **Fonts** and **Sizes.** Click on **Courier** and **12.**

ITALICS AND UNDERLINING

Prior to the invention of computers and word processing programs, writers used underlining to designate words which were to be italicized by the printer. Many colleges and universities still require such underlining and frown on the use of italics in formal papers. You should discuss this matter with your instructor if you wish to use italics.

Foreign words and the titles of books, magazines, and newspapers are underlined to indicate italics.

1. Select the text you want to italicize.
2. Choose **Font** from the **Format Menu.** The **Font Dialog Box** will appear.
3. Choose **Italic** from the **Font Style scrollable list.**
4. Click on **OK.**
5. Select the text you want to underline.
6. Choose **Font** from the **Format Menu**.
7. Choose **Single** from the **Underline scrollable list.**
8. Click **OK.**

or

1. Select text. Click on the *I* or <u>U</u> buttons in the **Formatting Tool Bar.**

CENTERING AND JUSTIFYING

Justification describes how words are placed on the page: flush left, flush right, or centered. **Microsoft Word** allows you to spread the words on each line across the page so the right margin is straight or right justified. Although **MLA** papers should not be justified, you will need to center or move some text at times.

1. Select the text you want to center or move.
2. Click on the appropriate **Justification Button** just to the right of the **B, *I*, U Buttons** in the **Formatting Toolbar** to center or move text.

INDENTION

MLA papers are indented one half inch. The **Microsoft Word** default setting is one half inch, but you may want to change indents for quotations or other purposes.

1. Select the text for which you want to change indents.
2. Choose **Paragraph** from the **Format Menu.** The **Paragraph Dialog Box** will appear.
3. Change the **Left** and **Right Indentation** settings by typing in new settings or clicking on the **increase** or **decrease arrows.**
4. Click on **OK.**

PAGINATION

Beginning with the first page, **MLA** papers carry a right justified heading one half inch from the top of the page with your last name in upper and lower case followed by the page number in arabic numerals. **See sample pages on pages 4-19 through 4-22.**

1. Choose **Header** and **Footer** from the **View Menu.** The text will dim and the cursor will appear in the header space. The **Header and Footer Toolbar** will also appear.
2. Click the **Switch Between Header and Footer Button** which is the first button on the left in **Windows 7,** the **fourth button** from the right in **Windows 97, 98,** and **2000** to be sure you are in the header space.
3. Click the **Page Number Button** which has a number sign on an icon page with a folded corner in the **Header and Footer Toolbar.** The number **1** will appear at the left margin.

4. The cursor will appear just to the right of the number **1** at the left margin. Press the **Left Arrow Key** to move the cursor to the left of the number **1.**
5. Press the **Space Bar** three times to move the number **1** three spaces to the right.
6. Press the **Left Arrow Key** to move the cursor to the left margin.
7. Type your last name. The cursor will be at the last letter of your name.
8. Press the **Left Arrow Key** to move the cursor to the beginning of your name.
9. Click the **Right Justification Button** in the **Formatting Toolbar.** Your name and page number **1** will shift to the right margin.

TITLE PAGE

MLA papers do not have a formal title page. **Your name, instructor's name, course number,** and **date** are grouped at the upper left corner of the first page. See **sample Title Page** on **page 4-19.**

1. Move the cursor to the top line of the first page.
2. Type in upper and lower case, **your full name,** first name first, on the top line, the **instructor's name** on the second line, the **course number** on the third line, and the **date** on the fourth line, double spaced at the left margin.
3. Double space and center the **title** in upper and lower case. Double space and begin your paper.

AUTHOR-PAGE CITATIONS

MLA papers use a simple system of citing sources by stating the author's name and page number(s) of the work in parentheses. Citations are placed directly in the text. No special keystrokes are necessary. The citations lead readers to the alphabetical list of sources in the **Works Cited** list at the end of the paper. **Follow the explanation and examples of parenthetical citations on pages 4-2 through 4-4. See the sample Text Page with author-page citations on page 4-20.**

1. Citations are placed directly in the text. No special keystrokes are necessary.

WORKS CITED LIST

The **Works Cited** list is printed at the end of the paper and presents the full bibliographic information for every source cited in the body of your paper. Do not include sources you may have consulted, but did not use. It is a good idea to prepare the **Works Cited** list before you actually start the paper so you will know how to cite the references in the text. **See the sample formats for Works Cited entries on pages 4-5 through 4-14 and the sample Works Cited page on page 4-22.**

1. Move the cursor to the end of the last line of text. Press **Enter** to place the cursor on a new blank line.
2. Choose **Break** from the **Insert Menu.** The **Break Dialog Box** will appear.
3. Click on the **Page Break Button** and **OK.**

or

4. Press **Ctrl+Enter.**
5. Center the words, **Works Cited,** in upper and lower case on the top line. Double space.
6. Type entries in alphabetical order using the appropriate format for the type of reference you are citing. The first line of each entry begins at the left margin with following lines double spaced and indented a half inch.
7. Double space within and between entries.

TABLES

Tables should be used sparingly. Use them only when data will be better presented in tabular form. Avoid confusing the reader by breaking up text with too many tables. Do not duplicate information in the text which appears in a table. A table should supplement material in the text, but it should also be understandable alone.

Tables are assigned arabic numerals and brief titles and are located as close as possible to their mention in the text. Every column must have a short heading. The data in the left column usually describes the major independent variable.

Use horizontal rules only and use vertical spacing to make the table easily readable. Double space within tables. **See the sample Table on page 4-21.**

Although **Microsoft Word 6** and **7** have programs to set up tables automatically, **MLA** tables are very simple with no vertical rules and only a few horizontal rules. The easiest and quickest way to prepare tables is with tabs.

1. Move the cursor to the place in the text where the table will be inserted. Leave three blank lines.
2. Type, **Table 1**, flush left without a period.
3. Double space and type the **title** flush left in upper and lower case. Extra lines of title are centered and double spaced.
4. Double space and type a **line of hyphens** across the page.
5. You must now set up the rows and columns which make up the table. Each column must have a header and these should be spaced evenly across the top of the table. The first column of the table is at the left margin. The last column should be near the right margin.

Setting Tabs for Headers

6. Type the **first header** flush with the left margin. Capitalize the first letters of major words in each heading.
7. Look at the extreme left end of the ruler. You will see a **Tab Alignment Button** with an **L-shaped marker.** Each time you click on it the marker will change to an **upside down T**, a **backwards L**, or an **upside down T with a dot** . The **L-shape** is the **Tab Alignment Button** for **aligning text at the left letter**, the **upside down T** is for **centering text at the tab**, the **backwards L** is for **aligning text at the right letter**, and the **upside down T with a dot** is for **aligning numbers at a decimal point.**
8. Click on the **Tab Alignment Button** until it changes to the **upside down T.**
9. Click in the ruler to set a tab at the approximate location where the second header should be. Continue the process by clicking in the ruler at the approximate locations where each header should be.
10. Press the **Tab Key** and type the second header. It will be centered at the tab location. Follow the same procedure with the remaining headers. If the spacing doesn't look right, select a header you would like to move, click on its **Tab** and drag it left or right until the spacing looks correct. The headers will move with the **Tabs** as you move them.
11. Double space and type a line of hyphens under the headers.

Entering Data

12. Double space and enter data in each column by pressing the **Tab Key** to move the cursor to the next column. Double space between rows.

13. If you are entering decimal data, click on the **Tab Alignment Button** until it changes to an **upside down T with a dot**. Decimal data entered will be aligned on the decimal points.

14. Double space after entering data and type a line of hyphens.

Reset Default Tab Settings

15. Choose **Tabs** from the **Format Menu**. The **Tabs Dialog Box** will appear. Click **Clear All**. The tabs you set for the table will disappear.

16. Use the **Up** and **Down Arrows** to set **.5"** in the **Default Tab Stops Box**. Click **OK**. The default tabs will be set.

17. Double space and continue typing your document.

SPELL CHECK

Word 6 - Word 7 - Word 97- Word 2000

1. Choose **Spelling** from the **Tools Menu**. The **Spelling Dialog Box** will open.

2. Misspelled words will appear in the **Not in Dictionary Box** with the correctly spelled word in the **Change to** or **Suggestions Box**. Other variations of the word will appear in the **Suggestions Scroll Box**.

3. If the correct word is in the **Change to Box**, click **Change** or **Change All** to correct the word wherever it appears in the paper.

4. If the word you want is in the **Suggestions Scroll List**, click on it and then click **Change**.

5. If the word is correctly spelled as is, and **Word's Spell Check** does not recognize it, click **Ignore.**

Word 7 - Word 97 - Word 2000   Automatic Spell Checking

Word will place a ragged, red underline under misspelled words as you type.

1. Choose **Options** from the **Tools Menu**. Choose the **Spelling and Grammar Tab** and be sure there is a check on the **Automatic Spell Checking** or **Check Spelling as You Type option**. If not, click on it.

2. Click the **right mouse button** on the misspelled word. A list of **replacement words** will appear.

3. Click on the **correct replacement word** or click **Ignore All**. If it is a special word, click on **Add** to add the word to the **dictionary**.

PRINTING

Word 6

1. Choose **Print** from the **File Menu**. The **Print Dialog Box** will appear.
2. If you are using your computer in a lab and there are several printers, click on **Printer** to be sure you are using the correct printer. The **Print Setup Dialog Box** will appear showing the **Default Printer**. If it is the correct printer, click on **Cancel**. If not, click on the correct printer in the **Printers Scroll List** and click on **Set as Default Printer**. The **Print Dialog Box** will reappear.
3. Be sure **Document** is displayed in the **Print What** list. Use the **Up** or **Down Arrows** in the **Copies Box** to select the number of copies you want to print. Click on one of the **Buttons** in the **Page Range Box**. If you want to print selected pages, separate individual pages by commas and series of pages by a hyphen. For example, if you type: 5, 9-12, 15 the printer will print pages 5, 9, 10, 11, 12, and 15.

Word 7 - Word 97 - Word 2000

1. Choose **Print** from the **File Menu**. The **Print Dialog Box** will appear.
2. If you are using your computer in a lab and there are several printers, click on the down arrow at the right end of the **Printer Box**. All available printers will be displayed. Click on the correct printer.
3. Be sure **Document** is displayed in the **Print What list**. Use the **Up** or **Down Arrows** in the **Number of Copies Box** to select the copies you want to print. Click the **Down Arrow** in the **Print Box** if you want to print a range of pages. If you want to print selected pages, separate individual pages by commas and series of pages by a hyphen. For example, if you type: 5, 9-12, 15 the printer will print pages 5, 9, 10, 11, 12, and 15.

SAVING

Word 6

1. Choose **Save** from the **File Menu** or click the **Save Button** in the **Standard Toolbar**. It is the third button from the left and has a picture of a floppy disk on it. The first time you save a document, **Word** will open the **Save As Dialog Box**.
2. The **Insertion Point** will be blinking in the **File Name Box**. Type the name of your document. It may have no more than 8 characters and no commas, periods, or spaces. **Word** will assign an **extension** of three characters called **doc**.
3. Check that **drive C** is selected in the **Drives: Box**. This is the usual designation for the hard drive.
4. Choose a **Directory** where you want to save your document in the

Directories: Scroll List. Winword is as good a directory as any.

5. Click on **OK.**

6. To avoid disaster, click on the **Save Button** in the **Standard Toolbar** every ten or fifteen minutes. **Word** will save your work instantly to the hard drive and directory you selected in the **Save As Dialog Box.**

7. An easy way to save your work is to turn on **Automatic Save.** Click on the **Options Button** in the **Save As Dialog Box.** Enter the interval in minutes in the **Automatic Save Every Box.** Ten minutes is good for most people. Type **10.**

8. It is a good idea to save your document on another disk just in case the hard drive crashes or some other glitch which computers are known for develops. Choose **Save As** from the **File Menu.** The **Save As Dialog Box** will appear.

9. Insert a **floppy disk** in the **floppy drive.** Use the **down arrow** in the **Drives Scroll List** until the **A: Drive** appears.

10. Click **OK.** Your document will be saved on the floppy disk. Remove it and keep it in a safe place. Repeat the process when you finish working each day.

Word 7- Word 97 - Windows 2000

1. Choose **Save** from the **File Menu** or click the **Save Button** in the **Standard Toolbar.** It is the third button from the left and has a picture of a floppy disk on it. The first time you save a document, **Word** will open the **Save As Dialog Box.**

2. Select the disk and folder in which you want to save your document in the **Save in: Box.**

3. Type the name of your document in the **File Name Box. Word 7** and **Word 97** allows you to use up to **255** characters. **Word** will assign an **extension** of three characters called **doc.**

4. Click on **Save.**

5. To avoid disaster, click on the **Save Button** in the **Standard Toolbar** every ten or fifteen minutes. **Word** will save your work instantly to the folder and disk you selected in the **Save As Dialog Box.**

6. An easy way to save your work is to turn on **Automatic Save.** Click on Tools and General **Options** in the **Save As Dialog Box.** Enter the interval in minutes in the **Automatic Save Every Box or the Auto Recover Info Every: in Windows 2000.** Ten minutes is good for most people. Type **10.**

7. It is a good idea to save your document on another disk just in case the hard drive crashes or some other glitch which computers are known for develops. Choose **Save As** from the **File Menu.** The **Save As Dialog Box** will appear.

8. Insert a **floppy disk** in the **floppy drive.** Select **A:** in the **Save in: drop down list.** Click **OK.**

Modern Language Association
Author-Page Citation
With Microsoft Works

OPENING MICROSOFT WORKS FIRST TIME

Windows 3. 1 - Works 3. 0

1. At the **DOS** prompt, **C:\>** type win and press **Enter.** The **Program Manager Window** will appear with several icons.
2. Double click on the the **Microsoft Works group icon.** The **Works group window** will open.
3. Double click on the **Microsoft Works icon**. The **Startup Dialog Box** will appear.
4. Click on **Word Processor.** A blank **Microsoft Works Document Window** will appear similar to the one shown below with a **Menu Bar and Toolbar.** The cursor or insertion point will be flashing at the left margin. You are ready to being typing your paper.

Windows 95, 98, and 2000 - Works 4. 0

1. Click on the **Start Button** in the lower left corner of your screen.
2. Drag the pointer up to **Programs.** The **Programs Menu** will pop up.
3. Drag the pointer to **Microsoft Works 4. 0.** Another **Menu** will pop up. Drag the pointer to **Microsoft Works 4. 0.** The **Works Task Launcher** will open.
4. Click on the **Works Tools Tab** at the upper right corner. Click on **Word Processor.** A blank **Works Document Window** will open similar to the one shown below with a **Menu Bar**, **Toolbar**, **Title Bar** and **Ruler.** The cursor or insertion point will be flashing at the left margin. You are ready to begin typing your paper.

MICROSOFT WORKS 4. 0 DOCUMENT WINDOW

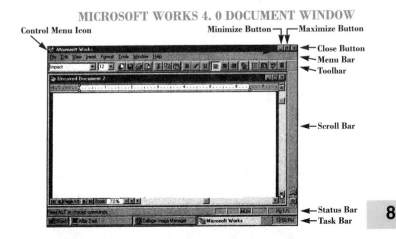

Control Menu Icon   Minimize Button   Maximize Button
Close Button
Menu Bar
Toolbar
Scroll Bar
Status Bar
Task Bar

OPENING YOUR DOCUMENT LATER

Windows 3. 1 Works 3. 0

1. Follow the steps above to open **Microsoft Works.**
2. Choose **Open Existing File** from the **Startup Dialog Box.**
3. Click on the file which you have named for your paper in the **File Name List** in the **Open Dialog Box.** Click **OK.** The **Document Window** will open with your paper.

Windows 95, 98, and 2000 – Works 4. 0

1. Follow the steps above to open **Microsoft Works.**
2. Choose **Open** from the **File Menu.**
3. Click on the file which you have named for your paper in the **File List.** If it is not there, use the **Down Arrow** to scroll through the **Look In Box** to locate the folder in which you saved your document.

MICROSOFT WORKS
Margins

MARGINS

The setting for **MLA** papers is one inch on top, bottom, and sides. You can change the margins if required by your instructor, but do not right justify or hyphenate words.

1. Choose **Page Setup** from the **File Menu.** The **Page Setup Dialog Box** will appear.
2. Choose the **Margins Tab** and enter **1"** in the **Top, Bottom, Left Margin,** and **Right Margin Boxes.**
3. Click **OK.**

LINE SPACING

MLA papers are double spaced throughout. The default setting for **Microsoft Works** is single spacing. Change the setting before you begin typing.

Works 3. 0
1. Choose **Paragraph** from the **Format Menu**. The **Paragraph Dialog Box** will appear.
2. Click on the **Breaks** and **Spacing Tab**.
3. Enter **2** in the **Between Lines Box** and click **OK**.

Works 4. 0
1. Choose **Paragraph** from the **Format Menu**. The **Paragraph Dialog Box** will appear.
2. Click on the **Spacing Tab** and use the **Up Arrow** in the **Line Spacing Box** to change the setting to **2 li.**
3. Click **OK.**

FONT

Font is the term used to describe the shape of the type used in typing. The **MLA** suggests using a standard typeface in 10 or 12 point size similar to that found in typewriters. **Courier** and **Times Roman** are good examples. Although **Microsoft Works** enables you to change the font, the size, and a whole range of styles such as bold, condensed, and shadow, select one simple typeface and keep it in the plain text style.

```
This is 12 point Courier font.
```

1. Click on the **Font Pop-up Menu** in the **Tool Bar**. Drag down to **Courier** or **Times New Roman.**
2. Click on the **Type Size Pop-up Menu** in the **Tool Bar**. Drag down to **12.**

MICROSFT WORKS
Line Spacing - Font

ITALICS AND UNDERLINING

Prior to the invention of computers and wordprocessing programs, writers used underlining to designate words which were to be italicized by the printer. Many colleges and universities still require such underlining and frown on the use of italics in formal papers. You should discuss this matter with your instructor if you wish to use italics.

Foreign words and the titles of books, magazines, and newspapers are underlined to indicate italics.

1. Select the text you want to underline or italicize.
2. Click on the *I* or U buttons in the **Tool Bar.**

CENTERING AND JUSTIFYING

Justification describes how words are placed on the page: flush left, flush right, or centered. **Microsoft Works** allows you to spread the words on each line across the page so the right margin is straight or right justified. Although **MLA** papers should not be justified, you will need to center or move some text at times.

1. Select the text you want to center or move.
2. Click on the **Left, Right** or **Center Justification Buttons** in the **Toolbar.** The are just to the right of the **B, *I*, U, Buttons.**

or

3. Press **Ctrl+L** to align left, **Ctrl+E** to center, **Ctrl+R** to align right, or **Ctrl+J** to justify.

INDENTION

MLA papers are indented one half inch. The **Microsoft Works** default setting is one half inch, but you may want to change indents for quotations or other purposes.

1. Choose **Paragraph** from the **Format Menu.** The **Paragraph Dialog Box** will appear.
2. Click on the **Indents** and **Alignment Tab.**
3. Enter **.5"** in the **First Line Indent Box.**
4. Enter any other changes you need in the **Left, Right,** and **First Line** boxes.
5. Click on **OK.**

PAGINATION

Beginning with the first page, **MLA** papers carry a right justified heading one half inch from the top of the page with your last name in upper and lower case followed by the page number in arabic numerals. **See sample pages on pages 4-19 through 4-22.**

1. Choose **Headers** and **Footers** from the **View Menu.** The **Headers** and **Footers Dialog Box** will open.
2. Type an **ampersand** and **small r** like this (**&r**) followed by your **last name.** Press the **space bar** three times to move the cursor three spaces to the right and type an **ampersand** and a **small p** like this (**&p**).
3. Click OK. The header will contain your name and page number at the right margin.
4. Click on **Print Preview** in the **File Menu** to see how the header looks on the page.

TITLE PAGE

MLA papers do not have a formal title page. **Your name, instructor's name, course number,** and **date** are grouped at the upper left corner of the first page. **See sample Title Page on page 4-19.**

1. Move the cursor to the top line of the first page.
2. Type in upper and lower case, **your full name,** first name first, on the top line, the **instructors's name** on the second line, and the **course number** on the third line, and the **date** on the fourth line, double spaced at the left margin.
3. Double space and center the **title** in upper and lower case.
4. Double space and begin your paper.

MICROSOFT WORKS
Title Page - Citations

AUTHOR-PAGE CITATIONS

MLA papers use a simple system of citing sources by stating the author's name and page number(s) of the work in parentheses. Citations are placed directly in the text. No special keystrokes are necessary. The citations lead readers to the alphabetical list of sources in the **Works Cited** list at the end of the paper. **Follow the explanation and examples of parenthetical citations on pages 4-2 through 4-4. See the sample Text Page with author-page citations on page 4-20.**

1. Citations are placed directly in the text. No special keystrokes are necessary.

WORKS CITED LIST

The **Works Cited** list is printed at the end of the paper and presents the full bibliographic information for every source cited in the body of your paper. Do not include sources you may have consulted, but did not use. It is a good idea to prepare the **Works Cited** list before you actually start the paper so you will know how to cite the references in the text. **See the sample formats for Works Cited entries on pages 4-5 through 4-14 and the sample Works Cited page on page 4-22.**

1. Move the cursor to the end of the last line of text. Press **Enter** to place the cursor on a new blank line.
2. Choose **Page Break** from the **Insert Menu**. A dotted line will appear across the page with a new page symbol. The status bar at the bottom of the screen will indicate the next page number.
3. Center the words, **Works Cited**, in upper and lower case on the top line. Double space.
4. Type entries in alphabetical order using the appropriate format for the type of reference you are citing. The first line of each entry begins at the left margin with following lines double spaced and indented one half inch. Double space between entries.

TABLES

Tables should be used sparingly. Use them only when data will be better presented in tabular form. Avoid confusing the reader by breaking up text with too many tables. Do not duplicate information in the text which appears in a table. A table should supplement material in the text, but it should also be understandable alone.

Tables are assigned arabic numerals and brief titles and are located as close as possible to their mention in the text. Every column must have a short heading. The data in the left column usually describes the major independent variable.

Use horizontal rules only and use vertical spacing to make the table easily readable. Double space within tables. **See the sample Table on page 4-21.**

Although **Microsoft Works** has a program to set up tables automatically, **MLA** tables are very simple with no vertical rules and only a few horizontal rules. The easiest and quickest way to prepare tables is with tabs.

1. Move the cursor to the place in the text where the table will be inserted. Leave three blank lines.
2. Type **Table 1** flush left in upper and lower case without a period on the top line.
3. Double space and type the **title** flush left in upper and lower case. Capitalize only the first letters of major words. Extra lines of title are flush left and double spaced.
4. Double space and type a line of hyphens across the page.
5. You must now set up the rows and columns which make up the table. Each column must have a header and these should be spaced evenly across the top of the table. The first column of the table is at the left margin. The last column should be near the right margin.

Setting Tabs for Headers

6. Type the **first header** flush with the left margin. Capitalize the first letters or major words in each heading.
7. Double click the **Arrow Pointer** on any **Tab** in the **Ruler**. The **Tabs Dialog Box** will open. Click on **Center** in the **Alignment Box**. Since no leaders are necessary, click on the **None Button** under **Leader.**
8. Look at the ruler and decide where you think the second header should be. For example, you might think it would look right at the two inch mark. Click the **Arrow Pointer** in the **Ruler** at the two inch mark. A **Center Tab Stop** will be placed at that position.
9. Continue the process for each of the headers you need.
10. Press the **Tab Key** and type the second header. It will be centered at the tab location. Follow the same procedure with the remaining headers.
11. Check the spacing to see if the headers are properly spaced. Make adjustments by selecting the header you want to move and dragging its **Tab Stop** to a new location on the ruler. The header will be dragged along with the **Tab Stop**. A bit of trial and error will give you the best spacing in a couple of minutes.
12. Double space and type a line of hyphens across the page.

Entering Data

13. Double space and enter numerical data in each column by pressing the **Tab Key** to move the cursor to the next column. Double space between each line of data. If any numerical data contains decimal points, reopen the **Tabs Dialog Box** and click the **Decimal Alignment Button** to line up decimal points in the data.
14. After entering data, double space and type a line of hyphens across the page.

Resetting Default Tab Settings

15. Double space to place the cursor on a new line. Choose **Tabs** from the **Format Menu**.
16. Click on **Delete All** and **OK**. The **Default Tab** settings of .5 inches will be set.
17. Double space and continue typing your document.

SPELL CHECK

1. Move the cursor to the top line of the first page of your paper.
2. Choose **Spelling** from the **Tools Menu** or click on the **Spelling Button** in the **Toolbar**. It's on the right end of the **Toolbar** and has the letters ABC with a check mark. The **Spelling Dialog Box** will open.
3. **Works** will display the first word which is not in its dictionary next to **Not in Dictionary:** and highlight the word in the **Change To: Box** and in your document.
4. Click on the **Suggest Button** and **Works** will list some suggested changes in the **Suggestions List Box**.
5. Click on the correct spelling in the **Suggestions List Box** and it will appear in the **Change To: Box**.
6. Click on the **Change Button** and the correct word will replace the incorrect spelling in the document. If you wish to change the word every time it appears, click on the **Change All Button.**
7. If the word is unusual or special and is correctly spelled even though it is not in the **Works** dictionary, click the **Ignore** or **Ignore All Button.** If you want to add the special word to the dictionary, click the **Add Button.** To save time, you can click the **Always Suggest Box** to save the step of clicking the **Suggest Button** each time.

PRINTING

1. Choose **Print Preview** from the **File Menu** or click on the **Print Preview Button** on the **Toolbar.** It is the fourth button to the right of the **Font Size Scroll Button.** It has a picture of a folded sheet of paper with a magnifying glass. The document will appear exactly as it will when printed. If you see any errors in spacing or layout, you can make adjustments by returning to the page in the regular view.
2. Choose **Printer Setup** from the **File Menu.** The **Printer Setup Dialog Box** will appear.
3. Use the **Scroll Bars** to view the available printers and click on the one you want to use. Click on **Setup** to change any values necessary. Click on **OK.**
4. Choose **Print** from the **File Menu.** The **Print Dialog Box** will open.
5. Make necessary changes in the **Number of Copies** and **Print Range Boxes.** Click on **OK.**

SAVING

1. Choose **Save As** from the **File Menu.** The **Save As Dialog Box** will open.
2. Type a file name for your document using no more than 8 characters without spaces in the **File Name Box.** The document will be saved to the hard drive, usually C:. Click on **OK.**
3. After you have named your document, choose **Save** from the **File Menu** or press **Ctrl + S** on the **Keyboard** every few minutes to avoid disaster.
4. It is a good idea to save your document to a floppy disk at the end of each session. Insert a formatted floppy in the A: drive.
5. Choose **Save As** from the **File Menu.**
6. Scroll down to the **A: drive** with the **Drives: Scroll Button.** Click on **OK.**

MICROSOFT WORKS
Printing - Saving

Part 3

Using the *Publication Manual of the APA* to Write Your Paper

Word Processing Applications

Part Three

Using the *Publication Manual of the APA* to Write Your Paper

Word Processing Applications

Chapter Nine

Author-Date Citation

Publication Manual of the American Psychological Association, 4th Ed.

The **American Psychological Association** has been publishing the ***Publication Manual*** since 1952. As the name of the organization implies, the ***Manual*** is primarily intended to guide writers and researchers in the field of psychology. However, writers in other disciplines have adopted the author-date citation method.

The fourth edition of the ***Publication Manual*** contains updated information on the preparation of papers as well as formats for citing electronic media such as CD-ROMs and electronic data bases. Particular attention has been given to the elimination of gender, racial, and socioeconomic bias in scientific writing.

PARENTHETICAL AUTHOR-DATE CITATION

The author's name and the date of the work are placed in parenthesis in the text. When the author's name appears in the text only the date needs to be placed in the parenthesis. A little practice may be necessary to insert the citation and keep the writing fluent. Author-date citation samples, single spaced to save space, are on pages 9-2 and 9-3.

Every source cited in the text must be documented in a Reference List at the end of the paper. It is important that references be cited accurately to permit readers to find and use the sources. Reference samples, also single spaced to save space, are on pages 9-4 through 9-9.

Parenthetical citations may be placed anywhere in the sentence, but be sure to maintain a smooth writing style, inserting the citation at a natural pause in thought. When both the author's name and date appear in the parenthesis, separate them with a comma.

PARENTHETICAL AUTHOR-DATE CITATION

WORK - SINGLE AUTHOR

Insert last name of author and year of publication in parentheses in the text.

    A study of reactive inhibition (Smith,
    1979) indicated

or

If author's name appears in text, insert only the year of the work in parentheses.

    Smith's (1979) study of reactive inhibition
    indicated

In a second or later mention of same work within a paragraph, the year may be omitted if there will be no confusion.

    In his study of reactive inhibition, Smith
    also found

WORK - TWO AUTHORS

Mention of a work by two authors should always include both names separated by an *ampersand (&)* in the parentheses and the word, *and,* in the text.

    In an explanation of mental disorder,
    (Rogers & Phillips, 1978) described

    Rogers and Phillips (1978) studied mental
    disorder

WORK - MULTIPLE AUTHORS

First mention of a work by three or more authors should include all the authors separated by an *ampersand (&)* in the parenthesis and the word, *and,* in the text.

    Published studies which illustrate the P
    technique (Cattel, Cattel & Rhymer, 1947)
    stress the relationship

    Published studies by Cattel, Cattel and
    Rhymer which illustrate the P technique

PARENTHETICAL AUTHOR-DATE CITATION

Later mention of a work by three or more authors. Cite only the last name of first author and the Latin abbreviation, et al., (not underlined and no period after et) and the year only if there is no confusion.

> In a study of P technique, Cattel et al.
> (1947) discovered

In a second or later mention of same work within a paragraph, the year may be omitted if there will be no confusion.

> Cattell et al. discovered

For a work with six or more authors, cite only the last name of the first author followed by et al. and the year for the first and subsequent citations. Use an *ampersand* (**&**) in the reference list.

> Smith, et al. (1996) investigated

Include initials of authors with the same last name

CORPORATE AUTHOR

The name of associations, government agencies, and organizations, should usually be spelled out in text at least at the first mention.

> Statistical reports on mental illness in
> the armed forces (National Institute of
> Mental Health [NIMH], 1989) indicated

Subsequent mention may be abbreviated if not confusing and if the reader can readily identify the source in the reference list.

> The study of mental illness (NIMH, 1989)
> indicated

WORK - NO NAMED AUTHOR

Use the first few words of the reference list entry which will probably be the title and date for the citation in the text.

> Latest study of the brain reveals new
> understandings of brain waves ("New Brain
> Study," 1995).

REFERENCES - BIBLIOGRAPHY

A bibliography called, References, printed on a separate page at the end of the paper, provides complete publication information for all of the sources cited in your paper. The citations in the text must lead the reader to the source in the Reference list. Entries are alphabetized letter by letter by author's last names, an association, or title if author is not known. Following are samples of reference citations.

APA REFERENCE SAMPLES

BOOKS

BOOK - NO AUTHOR

Psychology and you (1990). New York: Macmillan.

BOOK - ONE AUTHOR

Helmstadter, G. C. (1991). Research concepts in human behavior. New York: Houghton.

BOOK - MULTIPLE AUTHORS

Mathews, T. R., & Lawser, P. Q. (1993). Theories of management. New York: McGraw-Hill.

BOOK - CORPORATE AUTHOR

American Psychological Association. (1994). Publication manual of the American Psychological Association (4th ed.). Washington, DC: Author.

(When publisher and author are the same, use the word, Author, as name of publisher)

BOOK - MULTIVOLUME

Brosnia, R. (Ed.). (1989). Personality: Theory and practice (Vols. 1-4). New York: Macmillan.

BOOK - EDITOR INSTEAD OF AUTHOR

Feigenbaum, E., & Feldman, J. (Eds.). (1991). Computers and thought. New York: McGraw-Hill.

BOOK - REVISED EDITION

Robertson, J. (1989). Contemporary issues in psychology (Rev. ed.). New York: Praeger.

ARTICLE OR CHAPTER IN EDITED BOOK

Schwartz, R. P. (1990). Learning styles. In F.S. Keenan & L.F. Bird (Eds.), Education for the nineties (pp. 312-322). New York: Avon.

APA REFERENCE SAMPLES

DIAGNOSTIC AND STATISTICAL MANUAL OF MENTAL DISORDERS

American Psychiatric Association. (1994). Diagnostic and statistical manual of mental disorders (4th ed.). Washington, DC: Author.

ENCYCLOPEDIA ARTICLE - SIGNED

Johnson, R. S. (1994). Radioactivity. In The new encyclopedia Britannica (Vol. 25, pp. 453-455). Chicago: Encyclopedia Britannica.

ENCYCLOPEDIA ARTICLE - UNSIGNED

Somalia. (1993). In The new encyclopedia Britannica (Vol. 25, pp. 550-556). Chicago: Encyclopedia Britannica.

PERIODICALS

JOURNAL ARTICLE - ONE AUTHOR

Braverman, D. (1962). Normative and ipsative measurement in psychology. Psychological Review, 69, 295-305.

JOURNAL ARTICLE -TWO AUTHORS
JOURNAL PAGINATED BY ISSUE AND NUMBER

Roberts, J. R., & Smithson, B. (1975). Family orientations of Chinese college students. Journal of Marriage and the Family, 34(4), 29-37.

JOURNAL ARTICLE - THREE TO FIVE AUTHORS

Bronkowski, L. P., Johnson, R. J., Oppenheimer, K. S., & Pushkin, B. J. (1994). Age as a factor in flight training. Journal of Applied Psychology, 79, 421-427.

MAGAZINE ARTICLE

Horowitz, C. H. (1994, October 10). Is Rikers about to explode? New York, 27, 29-37.

NEWSPAPER ARTICLE - SIGNED

Barron, J. (1995, June 30). Brain studies give clues on depression. New York Times, pp. A1, A3.

NEWSPAPER ARTICLE - UNSIGNED

Gene seen as possible link to AIDS. (1996, August 10). The New York Times, p. A1.

APA REFERENCE SAMPLES

MONONOGRAPH WITH ISSUE NUMBER AND SERIAL OR WHOLE NUMBER

Coswell, R., & Klingenstein, P. R. (1965). A computer model of personality. Psychological Monographs, 79(1, Whole No. 540).

MONOGRAPH BOUND SEPARATELY AS JOURNAL SUPPLEMENT

Johnson, P. Q., & Pritchard, K. (1969). Creativity. Journal of Experimental Psychology Monographs, 80,(1, Pt. 2).

MONOGRAPH BOUND IN JOURNAL WITH CONTINUOUS PAGES

Hirsch, J., & Brown, R. W. (1974). Analysis of bias in selecting test times [Monograph]. Journal of Experimental Psychology, 98, 325-331.

REPORTS

GOVERNMENT PRINTING OFFICE REPORT

United States Public Health Service. (1990). Statistical tables for medical research (USPHS Publication No. 37). Washington, DC: U.S. Government Printing Office.

REPORT DIRECT FROM GOVERNMENT AGENCY

U.S. Department of Health and Human Services. (1994). Breast cancer: geographic studies (AHCPR Publication No. 94-0313). Rockville, MD: Author.

NATIONAL TECHNICAL INFORMATION SERVICE (NTIS) REPORT

Braveson, R. B., & Rogers, E. S. (1992). Authentic assessment and teacher variables. Ann Arbor: University of Michigan. (NTIS No. RS 93-721 215/KR)

EDUCATIONAL RESOURCES INFORMATION CENTER (ERIC) REPORT

Cook, J. V. (1992). Teaching styles (Report No. NCRTL-RJ-46-3). New York, NY: Center for Research on Teaching. (ERIC Document Reproduction Service No. ED 241 079)

APA REFERENCE SAMPLES

DOCTORAL DISSERTATIONS

DOCTORAL DISSERTATION IN DISSERTATION ABSTRACTS INTERNATIONAL OBTAINED FROM A UNIVERSITY

Baron, A. (1990). The use of personality factors as criteria for grouping pupils for computer instruction (Doctoral dissertation, New York University, 1990). Dissertation Abstracts International, 49, 4379A

DOCTORAL DISSERTATION IN DISSERTATION ABSTRACTS INTERNATIONAL OBTAINED ON UNIVERSITY MICROFILM

Baron, A. (1990). The use of personality factors as criteria for grouping pupils for computer instruction. Dissertation Abstracts International, 49, 4379A. (University Microfilms No. ABD72-13497)

UNPUBLISHED DOCTORAL DISSERTATION

Smeterna, C. K. (1993). Stuttering and its effects on academic achievement. Unpublished doctoral dissertation, University of Michigan, Ann Arbor.

REVIEWS

REVIEW OF BOOK, FILM, OR VIDEO

Shanahan, P. M. (1994). Challenging the giants [Review of the book Freud and Jung]. Contemporary Psychology, 39, 321-322.

AUDIOVISUAL SOURCES

TELEVISION - EPISODE FROM A SERIES

Place the name of the writer in author location. Place the name of the director in parentheses after the title. Place the name of the producer in the editor location.

Moyers, B. (1995). The field of time (D. Grubin, Director). In R. Rogers (Producer), The language of life with Bill Moyers. New York: WNET.

APA REFERENCE SAMPLES

FILM-VIDEOTAPE-AUDIOTAPE-SLIDES-WORKS OF ART

Place the name of major contributors first, followed by their functions in parentheses. Place the medium in brackets after the title. Give the location and name of distributor.

Markson, J. (Producer), & Cohen, K. (Director). (1995). <u>The golden touch</u> [Film]. New York: MCA.

SOUND RECORDING

Place the name of major contributors first, followed by their function in parentheses. Place the medium in brackets after the title. Give the location and name of distributor.

Browning, R. Z. (Speaker). (1991). <u>Treatment of phobia</u> [Cassette Recording No. 419-212-79A-B]. Washington, DC: American Psychological Association.

CD-ROM - ELECTRONIC DATA TAPE - CARTRIDGE TAPE

Use the same formats for author, date, and title elements as print material. After title and before the period, insert in brackets the type of medium. Add location and name of producer..

Branson, T.J. (1996). <u>Astronomy Today</u> (2nd ed.) [CD-ROM]. New York: World Publishing.

ABSTRACT ON CD-ROM

Author. (Year). Title [CD-ROM]. <u>Journal Title Volume</u> (issue). Abstract from: Source and retrieval number

King, A. J. (1992). Longitudinal study of stuttering [CD-ROM]. <u>Journal of Applied Psychology, 77,</u> 410-417. Abstract from: SilverPlatter File: PsycLIT Item: 79-18421.

JOURNAL ARTICLE ON CD-ROM

Author. (Year). Title [CD-ROM]. <u>Journal Title Volume</u> (issue), paging or indicator of length. Supplier/Database name Identifier or number (if available).

Rogers, R.R. (1994, June). Perseveration in driving habits [CD-ROM]. <u>Journal of Applied Psychology 4</u>, 5-6. 1994 SIRS/SIRS 1994 Psychology/Volume 4/Article 12A

APA REFERENCE SAMPLES

INTERNET SOURCES

With the rapid expansion of electronic publishing, conventions for citing Internet references are revised periodically. The examples given here reflect the standards established by the APA in 1998. Any citation should let the reader know as much bibliographic information as possible and enable him or her to find the source. If both electronic and print versions are identical, the print form of citation is preferred.

Therefore, references should begin with all the data that would be provided for a print document. Place the Internet data at the end of the citation beginning with the words, Retrieved from, the date of access, and the Internet address (URL). The access date is important because electronic material may change, disappear, or move to a different site. If you need to divide a URL between two lines, do so only after a slash. Use no hyphen at the break.

E-MAIL
E-mail and information obtained in discussion groups or bulletin boards is not permanently available and should be cited as personal communication in the body of your paper, but not cited in the reference list.

R. King, (personal communication, March 26, 1998)

ON-LINE JOURNAL ARTICLE
Author. (Year). Title [Paging or indicator of length]. Journal Title [Type of medium], volume(issue). Retrieved Date from the World Wide Web: URL

Braverman, D. (1962). Normative and ipsative measurement in psychology [13 paragraphs]. Psychological Review 69. Retrieved January 26, 1998 from the World Wide Web: gopher:// panda1.uottowa.ca

ON-LINE JOURNAL ARTICLE - FILE TRANSFER PROTOCOL (FTP)
Rogers, R. R. (1993, June). Perseveration in driving habits [4 paragraphs]. Psycholoquy [On-line serial], 4(13). Retrieved January 15, 1995 from the World Wide Web: ftp://duke.edu/pub/ harnad/Psycholoquy/1993.Volume.3.volume.4. psycoloquy.93.4.13.base-rate.11.rogers

APA REFERENCE SAMPLES

ON-LINE MAGAZINE ARTICLE

Author. (Year, month day for weeklies - month for monthlies). Title. **Magazine Title, volume** (if given), paging or indicator of length. **Retrieved Date from the World Wide Web: URL**

Jones, M. (1996, October 16). Mid East peace? Time 41 paragraphs. Retrieved September 15, 1997 from the World Wide Web: http://www.time.com/jones.html

Gobel, Dave. (1998, April 1998). Distance Learning - Educating in Cyberspace. Online Magazine 22 paragraphs. Retrieved May 9, 1998 from the World Wide Web: http://www.online-magazine.com/lgu.html

ON-LINE NEWSPAPER ARTICLE

Author. (Year, month day). Title. **Newspaper Title, paging or indicator of length. Retrieved Date from the World Wide Web: URL**

Bradley, Ann. (1997, Mar 26). Educated Consumers. Education Week on the Web, 15 paragraphs. Retrieved April 4, 1998 from the World Wide Web: http://www.edweek.org/ew/vol-16/26consum.h16

ON-LINE EDITORIAL

Title [Editorial]. (Year, Month Day). **Newspaper Title**. Retrieved Date from the World Wide Web: URL

Small Schools as an Investment [Editorial]. (1998, May 1). New York Times on the Web. Retrieved May 20, 1998 from the World Wide Web: http://www.nytimes.com/yr/mo/day/editorial/01fri3.html

ON-LINE LETTER TO THE EDITOR (May be Untitled)

Author. (Year, Month Day). [Letter to the editor]. **Newspaper title**. Retrieved Date from the World Wide Web: URL

Harrison, Lawrence E. (1998, May 4). [Letter to the editor]. New York Times on the Web. Retrieved June 18 1998 from the World Wide Web: http://www.nytimes.com/yr/mo/day/letters/lharri.html

APA REFERENCE SAMPLES

PROFESSIONAL OR INSTITUTIONAL HOME PAGE
American Psychological Association Home Page. Retrieved May 7, 1998 from the World Wide Web: http://www.apa.org

ON-LINE BOOK
Author, (Year). Title. Publication Location: Publisher. Retrieved Date from the World Wide Web: URL
Conrad, Joseph, (1910). Heart of Darkness. New York: Harpers. Retrieved January 15, 1998 from the World Wide Web ftp://wiretap.area.com/Library/Classic/ darkness.txt

ON-LINE GOVERNMENT DOCUMENT
United States Department of State. (1998). Counter Terrorism Rewards Program. Retrieved February 21 1998 from the World Wide Web: http://www.heroes.net/pub/heroes/content2.html

ON-LINE ENCYCLOPEDIA
Author. (Date). Title. In Title of Encyclopedia. Publisher's location: Publisher. Retrieved Date from the World Wide Web: URL
James, William. (1897). The will to believe. In The internet encyclopedia of philosophy. New York: Longmans, Green and Company. Retrieved May 15, 1998 from the World Wide Web: http://www.utm.edu/research/iep/text/james/will/will.htm

ONLINE REVIEW (May be Untitled)
Author. (Date). Title [Review of the book Title] Name of On-line Program. Retrieved Date from the World Wide Web: URL
Bowen, Wayne H. (1988). [Review of the book Fascism: A history]. History Reviews On-Line 4. Retrieved September 5, 1988 from the World Wide Web:http://www.depauw.edu/dtrinkle/hrol/eatwell.html

APA QUOTATIONS

Quotations of 40 words or less:
Run into text and set off with double quotation marks. Place periods and commas within closing quotation marks. Place other punctuation inside quotation marks when they appear in the original material. Use single quotation marks for quotations within a quotation.

> Richardson (1996) found that "younger
>
> subjects learned three of the skills more
>
> rapidly than older subjects" (p. 29).

Quotations of more than 40 words:
Introduce the quotation by ending the preceding line with a colon. Double space and indent one half inch or five spaces from the left margin. Double space and type the quotation double spaced without quotation marks. If more than one paragraph is quoted, indent the first line of each an additional half inch or five more spaces. Do not use punctuation after the parenthetical reference.

> Richardson (1996) found the following:
>
> > The younger subjects learned color
> >
> > selection, timing, and manipulation at
> >
> > a much faster rate than the older
> >
> > subjects. The largest difference in
> >
> > learning rate occurred in the timing
> >
> > skill. (p. 29)

QUOTATION WITHIN A QUOTATION
Use single quotation marks to set off a quotation within a quotation.

ELLIPSIS
When omitting words, phrases or sentences from quoted material, use three periods with a space before the first and a space after the last. Type four periods to indicate an ellipsis between two sentences. One period will end the sentence and be followed by three periods.

Among soldiers, some . . . succeed in

recording in prose or poetry the thrill and

horror of their experience, and their

personal reflections about war.

APA NUMBERS

· **Use words for numbers below 10, and use numerals for numbers 10 and above.**

    Three subjects   *Seven* experimental trials

· **Use numerals in numbers below 10 when comparing with numbers 10 and above.**

    5 of the *26* groups   *2* subjects in Group A
    failed compared with *16* subjects in Group B

· **Use numerals for numbers preceding measurement units.**

    frequency *121.5* megahertz   *6* cm

· **Use numerals in numbers representing mathematical functions.**

    the *3*rd decile   *3*%   *6* times as often

· **Use numerals in dates, ages, sums of money, subjects in experiments, page numbers, and chapter numbers.**

    June *2, 1996*   *5* year olds,   *$30.00*
    2 hrs   page *7*

· **Use words for *zero* and *one* when words are more understandable, and when not used with numbers 10 and above.**

    one-time usage   *zero* sum game

APA CAPITALIZATION

Capitalize the following:

First word in a complete sentence
> The members of the family met.

Major words in headings and titles in body of text.
> The novel, <u>Of Human Bondage</u>

Capitalize only the first word of titles in reference lists.
> Rogers, B. Q., (1995). Effects of aircraft noise on residents.

Proper nouns
> African-American

Nouns followed by numerals or letters
> Experiment 6
> Table 6

But not parts of books or tables
> chapter 6
> column 3

Test titles
> Scholastic Aptitude Test

Derived factors within a factor analysis
> Stress Factor 9

Variables and effects with multiplication signs
> the Speed x Time equation

But
> variables of speed and time

APA ABBREVIATIONS

Use abbreviations with care, understanding that overuse can cause confusion and uneven writing.

Abbreviate the following:
Common terms not listed as abbreviations in *Webster's Collegiate*

```
HIV, FBI, NASA, FDA
```

Terms frequently used in *APA Journals*

```
(MMPI) Minnesota Multiphasic Personality
       Inventory
(CR) conditioned response
(CS) conditioned stimulus
```

But do not abbreviate O, E, or S for observer, experimenter, or subject.

Measurement units with numeric values

```
44 cm, 121 Hz, 1300 ppm
```

Latin Abbreviations
Use Latin abbreviations in parenthetical copy and English translation in nonparenthetical copy.

```
e.g.,    for example    i.e.,    that is
vs.      versus         cf.      compare
```

Punctuation of abbreviations
Use periods with initials of names, U. S. as an adjective, Latin abbreviations, reference abbreviations.

```
A. J. Andrews   U. S. Army   i.e.   Vol. 2
```

Do not use periods with state names, capital letter and measurement abbreviations.

```
CA   PA   NIMH   APA   cm   hr
```

Plurals of abbreviations
Add an *s* without an apostrophe.

```
IRAs   Eds.   vols.
```

But form plural of page by writing `pp.`

SAMPLE APA TITLE PAGE

½"

2–3 word brief title ──────────────────────────► Workfare Effectiveness   1

◄──1"──►Running Head: EFFECTIVENESS OF WORKFARE IN THREE STATES

5 spaces

Abbreviated title—all caps
Not more than 50 characters
including punctuation and spaces

Center full title on page ───► Effectiveness of Workfare Programs in

Double space   Wisconsin, Delaware, and California from 1992 to 1994

Your name

Double space   Roger P. Quarles ◄──────────────

Your school

Michigan State University ◄──────────

SAMPLE APA ABSTRACT PAGE

1″ Workfare Effectiveness 2

½″

5 spaces

Abstract

Republicans and Democrats have mounted an attack on the current welfare system in the United States. Despite the humanistic motivation of the Great Society programs the efforts to end poverty have failed. Moreover, it is thought that the war on poverty has produced the opposite effect. The decline of family life, the increase in out of wedlock births to juveniles, and generational dependence on welfare benefits are the bitter fruit of the nation's long range goals. Despite the rhetoric espoused by both parties, Congress has been unable to act on any major reforms, preferring instead to allow the states to experiment with a range of workfare reforms. Even so, the results appear to fall far short of the simplistic goals of welfare reform.

1″ 1″

Type in single paragraph
No indention
Do not exceed 960 characters
including punctuation and spaces

APA MANUAL

SAMPLE APA FIRST TEXT PAGE

1″

½″

Workfare Effectiveness   3

Effectiveness of Workfare Programs in Wisconsin, Delaware, and

Full title centered →   California from 1992 to 1994

President Clinton pledged an "end to welfare as we know it" as part of the 1992 election campaign. However, the administration has been unable to get the Congress to act on the suggested reforms and, as a result, the states have proposed a wide range of experimental initiatives (Kellam, 1994). Several are based on the concept of workfare, a popular idea with both Republicans and Democrats.

When Congress passed the Jobs Opportunities and Basic Skills Program (JOBS) in 1988, it gave states matching funds to develop programs. Wisconsin, Delaware, and California are among the states which have begun workfare programs (Kellam, 1994). ← Author-date citation

←1″→ However, the picture is not altogether sanguine. Some critics of ←1″→ the workfare concept including Gilbert claim that workfare will increase welfare costs and simultaneously increase the numbers of homeless persons (1994). There are arguments that despite the faults of the old AFDC program fifty percent of recipients are off welfare within two years (Gilbert, 1994). Others state that a lack of funds for job training and child care will make workfare programs impossible to maintain. (Kaus, 1994).

Wisconsin's workfare program, often cited as a model, has not worked well for the clients or the employers say its critics (Conniff, 1992). The goal, simple as it sounds, to reduce dependence on welfare by putting people back on their feet, is obviously not as easy as it seems. Nevertheless, there have been

1″

SAMPLE APA TABLE

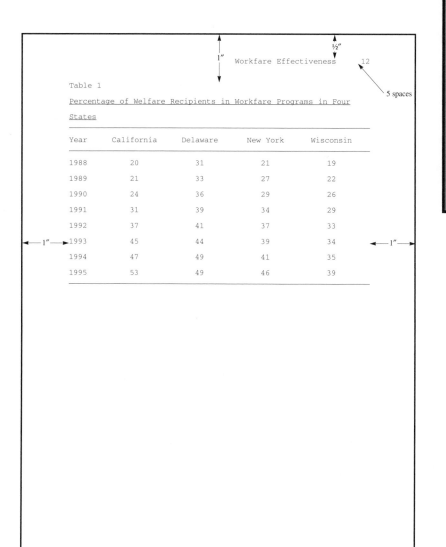

Workfare Effectiveness   12

Table 1

Percentage of Welfare Recipients in Workfare Programs in Four

States

Year	California	Delaware	New York	Wisconsin
1988	20	31	21	19
1989	21	33	27	22
1990	24	36	29	26
1991	31	39	34	29
1992	37	41	37	33
1993	45	44	39	34
1994	47	49	41	35
1995	53	49	46	39

5 spaces

APA TABLE

APA MANUAL

SAMPLE APA REFERENCE PAGE

Double space

References

Bernstein, P. R., Delanson, C. D., & Connelson, P. (1993). Attitudinal changes in mothers engaged in job training. *Journal of Applied Psychology, 78,* 452-457.

Carlson, R. J. (1994). *The dream and the dilemma: Welfare*

← 1″ → *in America.* New York: Macmillan.

Conniff, R. (1992, February). Cutting the lifeline: The real welfare fraud. *The Progressive,* 25-28.

← ½″ indent → Cowan, N. (1992, May-June). The big lie about workfare. *Utne Reader,* 28-29.

Gilbert, N. (1994, May) Why the new workfare won't work. *Commentary,* 47.

Kaus, M. (1994, April 25).s Tough enough: A promising start on welfare reform. *The New Republic,* 22-23.

Kellam, S. (1994, September 16). Welfare experiments: Are states leading the way toward national reform? *Congressional Quarterly Researcher,* 795-796.

Robinson, K., & Politcheck, B. R. (1994). *The politics of welfare reform.* New York: McGraw Hill

Schwartz, M. (1993). The role of the mother in AFDC families. *Consulting Psychology Journal: Practice and Research, 45*(4), 27-29.

U.S. Department of Health and Human Services. (1992). *Survey of Jobs Training Programs* (AHCPR Publication No. 92-0451). Rockville, MD: Author.

Workfare debate heats up in legislatures. (1993, August 21). *The Washington Post,* p. A3.

American Psychological Association
Author-Date Citation
With ClarisWorks 4.0 and 5.0

OPENING CLARISWORKS THE FIRST TIME

Windows 3. 1

1. At the **DOS** prompt, **C:\>**, type **win** and press **Enter.** The **Program Manager Window** will appear with several icons.
2. Double click on the **ClarisWorks Icon.** The **ClarisWorks Window** will appear.
3. Double click on **Word Processing.** A **Blank Document Page** will appear with the cursor flashing at the left margin.

Windows 95, 98, and 2000.

1. Click the **Start Button.** Choose **Programs,** the **ClarisWorks Folder,** and **ClarisWorks 4. 0** or **5.0 icon.** The **ClarisWorks New Document Dialog Box** will appear with **Word Processing** and **Create New Document** highlighted.
2. Click on **OK.** A **ClarisWorks Word Processing Document Window** similar to the one below will appear.

CLARISWORKS DOCUMENT PAGE WINDOW

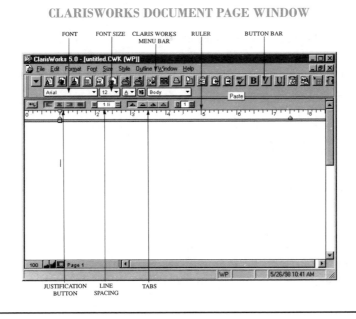

OPENING YOUR DOCUMENT LATER

1. Follow the steps above to open **ClarisWorks** from the **Program Manager Window** in **Windows 3. 1** or the **Start Button** in **Windows 95.**
2. Choose **Open** from the **File Menu** or click on the **Open File Button** in the **Default Button Bar.** The **Open Dialog Box** will appear.

ClarisWorks 4.0

3. Look for your document in the **File Name: list box.** If not there, click the down arrow next to the list box to scroll through the list until you see your document.

ClarisWorks 5.0

3. Look for your document in the list. If not there, click on the down arrow in the Look in Box to show the various drives. Click the drive or directory in which your document was saved.
4. Click on your document to highlight it and click **OK.** Your document will appear with the name in the **Title Bar.**

MARGINS

The setting for **APA** papers is one inch on top, bottom, and sides which is the default setting for **ClarisWorks.** You can change the margins if required by your instructor, but do not right justify or hyphenate words.

1. Choose **Document** in the **Format Menu.** The **Document Dialog Box** will open.
2. Type the modified margins in inches in each of the **Margins Boxes.**
3. Click on **OK.**

LINE SPACING

APA papers are double spaced throughout. The default setting for **ClarisWorks** is single spacing. Change the setting before you begin typing.

1. Click the **Increase Spacing Button** with two horizontal bars in the **Button Bar.** It is between the **Tabs** and **Justification Buttons.** The setting in the window will shift to **2 li.**

FONT

Font is the term used to describe the shape of the type used in typing. The **APA** suggests using a standard typeface in 12 point size similar to that found in typewriters. **Courier** and **Times Roman** are good examples. Although **ClarisWorks** enables you to change the font, the size, and a whole range of styles such as bold, condensed, and shadow, select one simple typeface and keep it in the plain text style.

```
This is 12 point Courier font.
```

1. Choose **Courier** in the **Font Menu or** in the **Pop-up Menu** in the **Button Bar.**
2. Choose **12 Point** in the **Size Menu or** in the **Pop-up Menu** in the **Button Bar.**

ITALICS AND UNDERLINING

Underlining is used to indicate words which are to be italicized in a printed version. Writers following **APA** style should not use italics unless approved by the instructor. The titles of books, periodicals, volume numbers in reference lists, some test scores, and Latin scientific terms are underlined to indicate italics.

1. Select the text you want to underline or italicize.
2. Choose **Underline** in the **Style Menu** or the **Pop-up Menu**, or click on the **U Button** in the **Button Bars.**
3. Choose **Italic** in the **Style Menu** or the **Pop-up Menu**, or click on the *I* **Button** in the **Button Bars.**

CENTERING AND JUSTIFYING

Justification describes how words are placed on the page: flush left, flush right, or centered. **ClarisWorks** allows you to spread the words on each line across the page so the right margin is straight or right justified. Although **APA** papers should not be justified, you will need to center or move some text at times.

CENTERING AND JUSTIFYING, continued.

1. Select the text you want to center or move.
2. Find the four **Justification Buttons** with several horizontal lines symbolizing lines of text under or over the ruler in the **Button Bar.**
3. Click on the **Center Justification Button** to center text.
4. Click on the appropriate **Justification Button** to move text left or right.

INDENTION

MLA papers are indented one half inch.

1. To change indentation in a paragraph, place the **cursor** in the paragraph.
2. Drag the **first line, left,** and **right indent markers** to the proper positions on the ruler. In ClarisWorks 4.0 the **first line indent marker** is a short horizontal line, the **left margin marker** is a right pointing triangle, and the **right margin marker** is a left pointing triangle. In ClarisWorks 5.0 the **first line indent marker** is a down pointing arrow, the **left margin marker** is an up pointing arrow, and the **right margin marker** is an up pointing arrow.
3. To indent the first line of a paragraph, drag the **first line indent marker** one half inch to the right of the **left margin marker.**
4. To change the left or right margins of the paragraph, drag the **left** and **right margin markers** to the appropriate position on the ruler.

PAGINATION

Beginning with the first page, **APA** papers carry a right justified heading one half inch from the top of the page with the first two or three words of the title of your paper in upper and lower case followed by the page number in arabic numerals. **See the sample pages on pages 9-16 through 9-20.**

1. Choose **Insert Header** from the **Format Menu.** A blinking cursor will appear at the left margin in a **Header box.**
2. Choose **Insert Page #** from the **Edit Menu.** Click **OK.**
3. The cursor will appear just to the right of the number 1 at the left margin. Press the **Left Arrow Key** to move the cursor to left of number 1.
4. Press the **Space Bar** five times to move the number 1 five spaces to the right.
5. Press the **Left Arrow Key** five times to move the cursor to the left margin.
6. Type the first two or three words of the title. The cursor will be at the last letter of the title.
7. Press the **Left Arrow Key** to move the cursor to the beginning of the title.
8. Click the **Right Justification Button** in the **Button Bar.** The title and page number 1 will shift to the right margin.
9. Click at the left margin of the first line of the text space under the header box to move the cursor there.

TITLE PAGE

APA papers have a specific format for the title page which contains a **running head,** the **title,** the **author's name,** and **affiliation. See sample title page on page 9-16.**

1. Move the cursor to the top line of the first page.
2. Type at the left margin the words, **Running Head:** in upper and lower case followed by a colon, leave one space and type, all in upper case, an **abbreviated title** of fewer than 50 characters including punctuation and spaces.
3. Center the **full title** in upper and lower case on the page. Double space if two or more lines.
4. Center **your name** in upper and lower case one double space below the title.
5. Center **your school name** in upper and lower case one double space below your name.

CLARISWORKS
Title Page

ABSTRACT PAGE

Formal **APA** papers include an **abstract page** which summarizes the paper. It is always numbered page 2. **See the sample Abstract Page on page 9-17.**

1. Move the cursor to the end of the last word in the **title page.**
2. Choose **Insert Break** from the **Format Menu.** The cursor will move to a new page which will be page 2.
3. Center the word, **Abstract**, in upper and lower case on the top line and double space.
4. Type the **abstract,** a summary of your paper, in a single paragraph without paragraph indention in fewer than 960 characters including punctuation and spacing.

TEXT

APA papers begin text on the third page. **See the sample Text Page on Page 9-18.**

1. Move the cursor to the last line in the abstract page. Press **Enter** to place the cursor on a new blank line.
2. Choose **Insert Break** from the **Format Menu.** The cursor will move to a new page which will be page 3.
3. Center the title of your paper in upper and lower case double spaced at the top of the page.
4. Double space and begin typing text.

AUTHOR-DATE CITATION

APA papers use a simple system of citing sources by stating the author's name and date of publication of the work in parentheses. Citations are placed directly in the text. No special keystrokes are necessary. The citations lead readers to the alphabetical list of sources in the **References** list at the end of the paper. **Follow the explanation and examples on pages 9-2 and 9-3.**

1. Citations are placed directly in the text. No special keystrokes are necessary.

REFERENCES LIST

The **References** list is printed at the end of the paper and presents full bibliographic information for every source cited in the body of your paper. Do not include sources you may have consulted, but did not use. It is a good idea to prepare the **References** list before you actually start writing the paper so you will know how to cite the references in the text. **See sample formats for References entries on pages 9-4 through 9-11 and the sample References Page on page 9-20.**

1. Move the cursor to the end of the last line of text. Press **Enter** to place the cursor on a new blank line.
2. Choose **Insert Break** from the **Format Menu.** The cursor will move to a new page.
3. Center the word, **References,** in upper and lower case on the top line. Double space.
4. Type entries in alphabetical order using the appropriate format for the type of reference you are citing.
5. Indent the first line of each entry one half inch. Double space within and between entries.

TABLES

Tables should be used sparingly. Use them only when data will be better presented in tabular form. Avoid confusing the reader by breaking up text with too many tables. Do not duplicate information in the text which appears in a table. A table should supplement material in the text, but it should also be understandable alone.

Tables are assigned arabic numerals and brief titles and are located as close as possible to their mention in the text on a separate page. Every column must have a short heading. The data in the left column usually describes the major independent variable.

Use horizontal rules only and use horizontal spacing to make the table easily readable. Double space within tables.

See the sample Table Page on page 9-19.

Although **ClarisWorks** has a program to set up tables automatically, **APA** tables are very simple with no vertical rules and only a few horizontal rules. The easiest and quickest way to prepare tables is with tabs.

1. Move the cursor to the end of the last line of text before the table to be inserted. Press **Enter** to move the cursor to a new blank line.
2. Choose **Insert Break** from the **Format Menu.** The cursor will move to a new page.
3. Type **Table 1** flush left in upper and lower case without a period on the top line.
4. Double space and type the **title** flush left and underlined. Capitalize only the first letters of major words. Extra lines of title are flush left and double spaced.
5. Double space and type a **solid line** across the page by pressing **Shift** and **Hyphen Keys.**
6. You must now set up the rows and columns which make up the table. Each column must have a header and these should be spaced evenly across the top of the table. Leave at least three spaces between columns.

Setting Tabs for Headers

7. Find the **four Tab Triangles** the **Button Bar.** One is **shaded** on the **left,** one on the **bottom,** one on the **right,** and one on the **top.** The one shaded on the left aligns columns on the left side of the tab, the one shaded on the bottom centers columns on the tab, the one shaded on the right aligns columns on the right side of the tab, and the one shaded at the top aligns columns of numbers along a decimal point.
8. Drag the **Center Triangle Tab Icon** to the approximate location on the ruler where the first header should be. Follow the same procedure for the remaining header locations.
9. Press the **Tab Key** to move the cursor to the first header location and type the header. Press the **Tab Key** and type the next header. Continue until all headers are typed. Capitalize only the first letter of the first word of each header.
10. Select any header and drag its **Triangle Tab Icon** left or right. The header will move with the icon to a new location. Use this method to adjust the locations of the headers until they are properly spaced.
11. Double space and type a **solid line** under the headers.

Entering Data

12. Enter data under each header by pressing tab to reach the next column. When you type the numbers to enter data, they will be centered under the **Tab Icons.** Be sure to align decimal points using the **Decimal Point Tab Icon.**
13. Double space and type a **solid line** across the page.
14. Double space and choose **Insert Break** from the **Format Menu.** The cursor will move to a new page. Continue typing your paper.

SPELL CHECK

1. Choose **Check Document Spelling** in the **Writing Tools Submenu** of the **Edit Menu** or click the **ABC Button** on the **Default Button Bar.** The **Spelling Dialog Box** will appear over the document window with misspelled words highlighted.
2. Click on one of the word options offered to correct it.
3. Click on **Replace** to replace the misspelled word with the correct one. Click on **Learn** if the word is a special use word not in the **Spell Check** dictionary.
4. Continue the process until the entire document been checked.

PRINTING

1. If you are using your computer in a lab and there are several printers, choose **Print Setup** from the **File Menu.** The **Print Setup Dialog Box** will appear. Choose the correct printer for your job.
2. Choose **Print** from the **File Menu** or click the **Print Button** on the **Default Button Bar.** The **Print Dialog Box** will appear. Change any other print settings as required. Click **Print** or **OK.**

SAVING

1. The first time you save a document choose **Save As** from the **File Menu.** The **Save As Dialog Box** will appear.
2. The **Cursor** will be blinking in the **File Name: Box.** Type the name of your document with no more than 8 characters in **ClarisWorks 3 & 4.**

ClarisWorks 3 and 4

3. **Drive C** is selected in the **Drives: Box** or you may change it.
4. Choose a **Directory** where you want to save your document in the **Directories Scroll List. Clworks** is usual or change it. Click **OK.**

ClarisWorks 5

3. The name of the folder in which you document will be saved will be in the **Save in: Box.**
4. Click on **Save.**
5. To avoid disaster, click on the **Save Button** in the **Standard Tool bar** every ten minutes. **ClarisWorks** will save your work instantly to the hard drive and directory you selected in the **Save As Dialog Box.**
6. It is a good idea to save your document on another disk just in case the hard drive crashes or some other glitch which computers are known for develops. Choose **Save As** from the **File Menu.** The **Save As Dialog Box** will appear.
7. Insert a **floppy disk** in the **A: Drive.** Use the **down arrow** in the **Drives Scroll List or the Save in: Box** until the **A: Drive** appears.
8. Click **Save** or **OK.** Your document will be saved on the floppy disk.

American Psychological Association

Author-Date Citation
With WordPerfect 6-7-8-9

OPENING WORDPERFECT THE FIRST TIME

Windows 3. 1

1. At the **DOS** prompt, **C:\>** type **win** and press **Enter.** The **Program Manager Window** will appear with several icons.
2. Double click on the **WPWin group icon** in the **Program Manager Window**. The **group icon window** will open.
3. Double click on the **WPWin 6 icon.**
4. A blank document window will appear similar to the one shown below with a **Menu Bar, Title Bar, Toolbar,** and **Power Bar.**
5. The cursor or insertion point will be flashing at the left margin.
6. You are ready to begin typing your paper.

Windows 95, 98 and 2000

1. Click the **Start Button.** Choose **Programs** and double click on the **WPWin 7, WPWin, and WpWin 9.**

WORDPERFECT DOCUMENT PAGE WINDOW

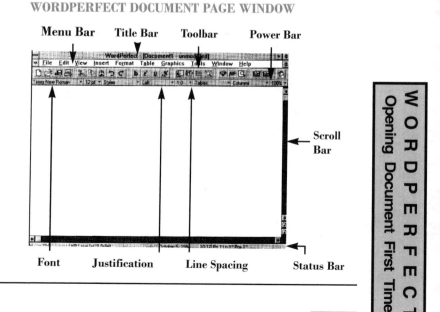

Menu Bar   Title Bar   Toolbar   Power Bar

Scroll Bar

Font   Justification   Line Spacing   Status Bar

OPENING YOUR DOCUMENT LATER

1. Follow the steps above to open **WordPerfect.**
2. Choose **Open** from the **File Menu** or click the **Open Button** in the **Toolbar.** It is the second button on the left and contains a picture of a file folder being opened. An **Open File Dialog Box** will appear.
3. Look for the name of your document in the **Filename: list box** in **WordPerfect 6, File List** in **WordPerfect 7,** or **Name text box in WordPerfect 8 or 9.** If you do not see the document, click the down arrow next to the list box to scroll through the list until you see your document name.
4. Click on your document to highlight it and click **OK** in **WordPerfect 6** or double click on your document in **WordPerfect 7, 8, or 9.** Your document will appear with the name in the **Title Bar.**

MARGINS

The setting for **APA** papers is one inch on top, bottom, and sides which is the default setting for **WordPerfect.** You must change the top margin to print the header containing the page number at the right location. You can change the margins if required by your instructor, but do not right justify or hyphenate words.

1. Choose **Margins** in the **Format Menu.** The **Margins Dialog** or **Page Set Up Box** will open.
2. Change the **Top Margin** to **.5"**
3. Make any other changes necessary.
4. Click on **OK.**

LINE SPACING

APA papers are double spaced throughout. The default setting for **WordPerfect** is single spacing. Change the setting before you begin typing.

1. Choose **Line** and **Spacing** from the **Format Menu.** A **Dialog Box** will appear.
2. Type **2** and click **OK.**

or

1. Click the **Line Spacing Button** in the **Toolbar** in **WordPerfect 7** or the **Property Bar** in **WordPerfect 8** and **9** and and click on **2.**

FONT

Font is the term used to describe the shape of the type used in typing. The **APA** suggests using a standard typeface in 10 or 12 point size similar to that found in typewriters. **Courier** and **Times Roman** are good examples. Although **WordPerfect** enables you to change the font, the size, and a whole range of styles such as bold, condensed, and shadow, select one simple typeface and keep it in the plain text style.

```
This is 12 point Courier font.
```

1. Choose **Font** from the **Format Menu.** The **Font Dialog Box** will appear.
2. Click the up or down arrows to scroll through the **Font Face: scroll list** until you locate **Courier** or similar font.
3. Click the **up** or **down arrows** to scroll through the **Font Size scroll list** until you reach **12.**
4. Be sure to click on **Regular** in the **Font Style drop down list.**
5. Click on **OK.**

or

1. Click on the **Font** and **Size Button**s in the **Power Bar** or **Toolbar.** Drop down lists will appear.
2. Click on **Courier** and **12.**

ITALICS AND UNDERLINING

Underlining is used to indicate words which are to be italicized in a printed version. Writers following **APA** style should not use italics unless approved by the instructor. The titles of books, periodicals, volume numbers in reference lists, some test scores, and Latin scientific terms are underlined to indicate italics.

1. Select the text you want to underline or italicize.
2. Choose **Font** from the **Format Menu.** The **Font Dialog Box** will appear.
3. Click **Underline** or **Italic** in the **Appearance Box.**
4. Click **OK.**

or

1. Select the text you want to underline or italicize.
2. Click on the **I** or **U Button** in the **Toolbar** or **Property Bar** in **WordPerfect 8** and **9.**

WORDPERFECT
Font   Italics

CENTERING AND JUSTIFYING

Justification describes how words are placed on the page: flush left, flush right, or centered. **WordPerfect** allows you to spread the words on each line across the page so the right margin is straight or right justified. Although **APA** papers should not be justified, you will need to center or move some text at times.

1. Select the text you want to center or move.
2. Click on the **Justification Button** in the **ToolBar** or **Property Bar in WordPerfect 8** and **9** and drag down to **Left, Center,** or **Right** as needed.

INDENTION

APA papers are indented one half inch. The **WordPerfect** default setting is one half inch, but you may want to change indents for quotations or other purposes.

1. Select the paragraph you want to indent.
2. Choose **Paragraph** in the **Format Menu.** The **Paragraph Format Dialog Box** will appear.
3. Change the **First Line Indent** by clicking on the up or down arrows.
4. Change the **Left** and **Right Margins** as required in the **Paragraph Adjustments Box.**
5. Click **OK.**

PAGINATION

Beginning with the first page, **APA** papers carry a right justified heading one half inch from the top of the page with the first two or three words of the title of your paper in upper and lower case followed by the page number in arabic numerals. **See sample pages on pages 9-16 through 9-20.**

WordPerfect 6 and 7

1. Be sure the cursor is on the first page of your paper.
2. Choose **Header/Footer** in the **Format Menu.** A **Header/Footer Dialog Box** will appear.

3. Choose **Header A** and **Create** in the **Headers/Footers Dialog Box.** A new window will open with the **name of your document** and **Header A** in the **Title Bar.** A **Feature Bar** with several buttons will be at the top of the window. The cursor will be flashing at the left margin.

4. Type **the first two or three words of the title** and press the **Space Bar five times** to leave five spaces after the short title.

5. Click on the **Number Button** in the **Features Bar.** The page number 1 will appear five spaces after the short title.

6. Click on the **Justification Button** in the **ToolBar** and drag down to **Right.** The header with the short title and page number will shift to the right margin.

7. Click on **Close.**

WordPerfect 8 and WordPerfect 9

1. Be sure the cursor is on the first page of your document.

2. Choose **Header-Footer** from the **Insert Menu.** A **Header-Footer Dialog Box** will appear.

3. Choose **Header A** and **Create** in the **Header-Footer Dialog Box.** The cursor will move to the **Header area** of the page. The words, **Header A**, will appear at the top of the screen next to your document name. Several buttons will be added to the **Property Bar.**

4. Type **the first two or three words of the title** and press the **Space Bar five times** to leave five spaces after the short title.

5. Click on the **Number Button** in the **Property Bar.** It is the button with a #1 in a box. The page number 1 will appear five spaces after the short title.

6. Click on the **Justification Button** in the **Property Bar** and drag down to **Right.** The header with your name and page number will shift to the right margin.

7. Click on **Close.**

TITLE PAGE

APA papers have a specific format for the title page which contains a **running head**, the **title**, the **author's name,** and **affiliation. See sample title page on page 9-16.**

1. Move the cursor to the top line of the first page.

WORDPERFECT
Pagination Title Page

2. Type at the left margin the words, **Running Head:** in upper and lower case followed by a colon, leave one space and type, all in upper case, an **abbreviated title** of fewer than 50 characters including punctuation and spaces.
3. Center the **full title** in upper and lower case on the page. Double space if two or more lines.
4. Center **your name** in upper and lower case one double space below the title.
5. Center **your school name** in upper and lower case one double space below your name.

ABSTRACT PAGE

Formal **APA** papers include an **abstract page** which summarizes the paper. It is always numbered page 2. **See sample Abstract Page on page 9-17.**

1. Move the cursor to the end of the last word in the **title page.** Press **Enter** to place the cursor on a new blank line.
2. Press **Ctrl + Enter** to begin a new page.
3. Center the word, **Abstract,** in upper and lower case on the top line and double space.
4. Type the abstract, a summary of your paper, in a single paragraph.without paragraph indention in fewer than 960 characters including punctuation and spacing.

TEXT

APA papers begin text on the third page. **See the sample Text Page on page 9-18.**

1. Move the cursor to the end of the last line of text on the **Abstract Page**. Press **Enter** to place the cursor on a new blank line.
2. Press **Ctrl + Enter** to begin a new page.
3. Center the **title** of your paper in upper and lower case double spaced at the top of the page.
4. Double space and begin typing text.

AUTHOR-DATE CITATIONS

APA papers use a simple system of citing sources by stating the author's name and date of publication of the work in parentheses. Citations are placed directly in the text. No special keystrokes are necessary. The citations lead readers to the alphabetical list of sources in the **References** list at the end of the paper. **Follow the explanation and examples on pages 9-2 and 9-3.**

1. Citations are placed directly in the text. No special keystrokes are necessary.

REFERENCES LIST

The **References** list is printed at the end of the paper and presents full bibliographic information for every source cited in the body of your paper. Do not include sources you may have consulted, but did not use. It is a good idea to prepare the **References** list before you actually start writing the paper so you will know how to cite the references in the text. **See sample formats for References entries on pages 9-4 through 9-11 and the sample References Page on page 9-20.**

1. Move the cursor to the end of the last line of text. Press **Enter** to place the cursor on a new blank line.
2. Press **Ctrl + Enter** to begin a new page.
3. Center the word, **References,** in upper and lower case on the top line. Double space.
4. Type the entries in alphabetical order using the appropriate format for the type of reference you are citing.
5. Indent the first line of each entry one half inch. Double space within and between entries.

TABLES

Tables should be used sparingly. Use them only when data will be better presented in tabular form. Avoid confusing the reader by breaking up text with too many tables. Do not duplicate information in the text which appears in a

WORDPERFECT
Citations References

table. A table should supplement material in the text, but it should also be understandable alone.

Tables are assigned arabic numerals and brief titles and are located as close as possible to their mention in the text on a separate page. Every column must have a short heading. The data in the left column usually describes the major independent variable.

Use horizontal rules only and use vertical spacing to make the table easily readable. Double space within tables. **See the sample Table on page 9-19.**

Although **WordPerfect** has a program to set up tables automatically, **APA** tables are very simple with no vertical rules and only a few horizontal rules. The easiest and quickest way to prepare tables is with tabs.

1. Press **Ctrl + Enter** to begin a new page.
2. Type **Table 1** flush left in upper and lower case without a period on the top line.
3. Double space and type the **title** flush left and underlined. Capitalize only the first letters of major words. Extra lines of title are flush left and double spaced.
4. Double space and type a **solid line** across the page by pressing **Shift** and **Underline Keys**.
5. You must now set up the rows and columns which make up the table. Each column must have a header and these should be evenly spaced across the top of the table. Leave at least three spaces between columns.

Setting Tabs For Headers

6. Choose **Ruler Bar** from the **View Menu**. The **Ruler** will appear with **Left Tab Stops** every half inch.
7. Place the cursor arrow in the bottom of the **Ruler** and click the **Right Mouse Button**. Drag down to **Clear All Tabs**. All the tab stops will disappear.
8. Click the cursor arrow in the bottom of the **Ruler**. Drag down to **Center**. This will change the **Left Tab Stops** to **Center Tab Stops** so all characters will be centered on the **Tab Stop**.
9. Place the cursor arrow in the bottom of the **Ruler** where you think the first header should be and click. A **Center Tab Stop** will be placed at the spot on the ruler.
10. Follow the same procedure for the remaining headers.

11. Type the headers moving the cursor with the **Tab Key**. Capitalize only the first letter of the first word of each header. If the spacing doesn't look right, select a header you would like to move, click on its **Tab Stop**, and drag it left or right until the spacing looks correct. The headers will move with the **Tab Stops** as you drag them.

12. Double space and type a solid line under the headers.

Entering Data

13. Double space and enter data moving the cursor with the **Tab Key**. If you want to enter decimal data, place the cursor arrow in the ruler, click the **Right Mouse Button**, and drag down to **Decimal**. Drag the **Center Tab Stop** off the **Ruler** and replace it with the **Decimal Tab Stop**. Decimal data entered will be aligned on the decimal points.

14. Double space after entering data and type a solid line.

Resetting Default Tab Settings

15. Double space and press **Ctrl + Enter** to start a new page.

16. To reset the **Default Tab Settings**, choose **Line** and **Tab Set** in the **Format Menu**. The **Tab Set Dialog Box** will appear. Click **Left** in the **Type Box**, **.500** in the **Position Box**, click on **Repeat Every .500**, and click **OK**.

17. Double space and press **Ctrl + Enter** to start a new page. Continue typing text.

SPELL CHECK

1. Move the cursor to the beginning of your paper.

2. Choose **Spell Check** from the **Tools Menu** or click the **Spell Check Button** in the **Toolbar**. It is on the right with an **Open Book icon**. The **Spell Checker or Writing Tools Dialog Box** will appear.

3. Click on options in the **Dialog Box** and be sure to choose all of the **Options** you want **Spell Checker** to do.

4. Click on **Start** if you have not selected **Auto Start** in **Options**.

5. **Spell Checker** will display the first misspelled word in the **Not Found: Box** and suggest a replacement word in the **Replace With: Box**. If the word is correct, click on **Replace**.

6. Other words will be suggested in the **Suggestions: List Box** in **WordPerfect 6** or in the **Replacements List Box** in WordPerfect 7, 8 and 9. Click on the **correct word** and **Replace**.

7. If your paper contains a word which is not in the dictionary, but which is correct, click on **Add** to add the word to the dictionary.

WORDPERFECT Spell Check

8. **WordPerfect 6** has a **Quick Correct** feature which is called **Spell as You Go** in **WordPerfect 7, 8** and **9.**

9. To start **QuickCorrect** in**WordPerfect 6**, choose **Quick Correct** in the **Tools Menu.** The **QuickCorrect Dialog Box** will appear. Click in the **Replace Words as You Type box.** If you misspell a word such as "the" for "the," **WordPerfect** will type it correctly.

10. To start **Spell as You Go** in **WordPerfect 7, 8** and **9,** choose **Proofread** and **Spell as You Go** from the **Tools Menu.** Misspelled words will be spelled correctly.

11. Misspelled words which are not in the dictionary will be marked with a **red underline. Right clicking** on the word will generate a drop down list of possible replacement words. Click on the **correct word** or click on **Skip in Document** if you want to ignore the misspelling or **Add** to add the word to the dictionary.

PRINTING

1. Choose **Print** from the **File Menu.**
2. Click on the selection you want to print in the **Print Selection Box** in **WordPerfect 6** or the **Print Box** in **WordPerfect 7, 8,** and **9.** In most cases, you will select **Full Document.**
3. Click on the number of copies and click **Print.**

SAVING

WordPerfect 6 - WordPerfect 7 - Wordperfect 8 - WordPerfect 9

1. The first time you save your document choose **Save As** from the **File Menu.** The **Save As Dialog Box** will appear.
2. Type a file name for your document using no more than 8 characters without spaces in the **File Name Box. WordPerfect 7, 8,** and**9. 8** allow you to use a name with up to 255 characters. The document will be saved to the hard drive, usually C:. Click on **OK.**
3. After you have named your document, choose **Save** from the **File Menu,** click on the **Save Button** in the **Toolbar,** or press **Ctrl+S** on the **Keyboard** every few minutes to avoid disaster.
4. It is a good idea to save your document to a floppy disk at the end of each session. Insert a formatted floppy in the A: drive.
5. Choose **Save As** from the **File Menu.**
6. Scroll down to the **A: drive** with the **Drives: Scroll Button.** Click on **OK.**

WORDPERFECT
Printing Saving

American Psychological Association
Author-Date Citation
Microsoft Word 6-7-97-2000

OPENING MICROSOFT WORD FIRST TIME

Windows 3. 1
1. At the **DOS** prompt, **C:\>**, type **win** and press **Enter**. The **Program Manager Window** will appear with several icons.
2. Look for either the **Microsoft Office icon** or the **Microsoft Word icon** If you see the **Microsoft Word icon**, double click on it. If you see the **Microsoft Office icon** first, double click on it and then double click on the **Microsoft Word icon**.
3. A blank **Microsoft Word Document Window** will appear similar to the one shown below with a **Menu Bar, Standard Toolbar, Formatting Toolbar, and** a **Ruler** under the **Menu Bar.**
4. The cursor will be flashing at the left margin.
5. You are ready to begin typing your paper.

Windows 95, 98, 2000
1. Click on the **Start Button** in the left corner of the **Taskbar**. Click on **Programs** and **Microsoft Word**. A blank **Word Document Window** similar to the one below will appear.

MICROSOFT WORD DOCUMENT WINDOW

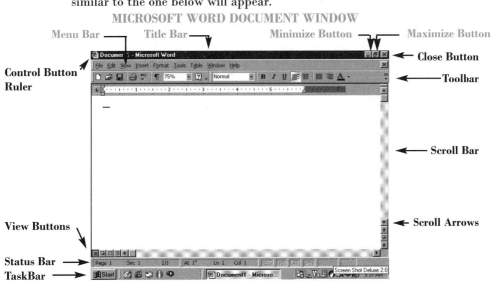

Menu Bar —— Title Bar —— Minimize Button —— Maximize Button

Control Button
Ruler

Close Button
Toolbar

Scroll Bar

Scroll Arrows

View Buttons

Status Bar ——
TaskBar ——

OPENING YOUR DOCUMENT LATER

1. Follow the steps above to open **Microsoft Word** from the **Program Manager Window** in **3.1** or the **Start Button** in **95, 98, and 2000.**
2. Choose **Open** from the **File Menu** or click the **Open Button** on the **Standard Toolbar.** It is the second button on the left and contains a picture of a file folder being opened. The **Open Dialog Box** will appear.
3. Look for the name of your document in the **File Name: list box** in **Word 6.** If you do not see the document, click the down arrow next to the list box to scroll through the list until you see your document name. Look in the **Look in: list box** in **Word 7** and **Word 97, 98, and 2000.** If you do not see your document, click on the **Up One Level Button** until you reach the folder you want to open.
4. Double click on your document. Your document will appear with the name in the **Title Bar**.

MARGINS

The setting for **APA** papers is one inch on top, bottom, and sides. You can change the margins if required by your instructor, but do not right justify or hyphenate words.

1. Choose **Page Setup** in the **File Menu.** The **Page Setup Dialog Box** will appear.
2. Click on the **Margins Tab** and type **1"** in each of the **Top, Bottom, Left, and Right boxes.**
3. Be sure the setting in the **From Edge** area is **0.5"** since this is the distance between the Header, which will appear with page numbers on every page, and the top edge of the page.
4. Click on **OK.**

LINE SPACING

APA papers are double spaced throughout. The default setting for **Microsoft Word** is single spacing. Change the setting before you begin typing.

1. Place the insertion point at the first line of your paper.
2. Choose **Paragraph** in the **Format Menu.** The **Paragraph Dialog Box** will open.
3. Choose **Double** from the **Line Spacing At: drop down list.**
4. Click **OK.**

FONT

Font is the term used to describe the shape of the type used in typing. The **APA** suggests using a standard typeface in 10 or 12 point size similar to that found in typewriters. **Courier** and **Times Roman** are good examples. Although **Microsoft Word** enables you to change the font, the size, and a whole range of styles such as bold, condensed, and shadow, select one simple typeface and keep it in the plain text style.

```
This is 12 point Courier font.
```

1. Click on the **Font** and **Size Buttons** in the **Formatting Toolbar.** Drop down lists will appear.
2. Click on **Courier** and **12.**

or

1. Choose **Font** from the **Format Menu.** The **Font Dialog Box** will appear.
2. Use the **up** and **down arrows** to scroll through the list of **Fonts** and **Sizes.** Click on **Courier** and **12.**

ITALICS AND UNDERLINING

Underlining is used to indicate words which are to be italicized in a printed version. Writers following **APA** style should not use italics unless approved by the instructor. The titles of books, periodicals, volume numbers in reference lists, some test scores, and Latin scientific terms are underlined to indicate italics.

1. Select the text you want to italicize.
2. Choose **Font** from the **Format Menu**. The **Font Dialog Box** will appear.
3. Choose **Italic** from the **Font Style scrollable list**.
4. Click on **OK**.
5. Select the text you want to underline.
6. Choose **Font** from the **Format Menu**.
7. Choose **Single** from the **Underline scrollable list**.
8. Click **OK**.

or

1. Select text. Click on the *I* or U buttons in the **Formatting Tool Bar**.

CENTERING AND JUSTIFYING

Justification describes how words are placed on the page: flush left, flush right, or centered. **Microsoft Word** allows you to spread the words on each line across the page so the right margin is straight or right justified. Although **APA** papers should not be justified, you will need to center or move some text at times.

1. Select the text you want to center or move.
2. Click on the appropriate **Justification Button** just to the right of the **B, *I*, U Buttons** in the **Formatting Toolbar** to center or move text.

INDENTION

APA papers are indented one half inch. The **Microsoft Word** default setting is one half inch, but you may want to change indents for quotations or other purposes.

1. Select the text for which you want to change indents.
2. Choose **Paragraph** from the **Format Menu.** The **Paragraph Dialog Box** will appear.
3. Change the **Left** and **Right Indentation** settings by typing in new settings or clicking on the **increase** or **decrease arrows.**
4. Click on **OK.**

PAGINATION

Beginning with the first page, **APA** papers carry a right justified heading one half inch from the top of the page with the first two or three words of the title of your paper in upper and lower case followed by the page number in arabic numerals. **See sample pages on pages 9-16 through 9-20.**

1. Choose **Header** and **Footer** from the **View Menu.** The text will dim and the cursor will appear in the header space. The **Header and Footer Toolbar** will also appear.
2. Click the **Switch Between Header and Footer Button** which is the first button on the left in **Windows 7** and the **fourth button** from the right in **Windows 97, 98** and **2000** to be sure you are in the header space.
3. Click the **Page Number Button** which has a number sign on an icon page with a folded corner in the **Header and Footer Toolbar.** The number 1 will appear at the left margin.
4. The cursor will appear just to the right of the number 1 at the left margin. Press the **Left Arrow Key** to move the cursor to the left of the number 1.
5. Press the **Space Bar** five times to move the number 1 five spaces to the right.
6. Press the **Left Arrow Key** to move the cursor to the left margin.
7. Type the first two or three words of the title of the paper. The cursor will be at the last letter of the title.
8. Press the **Left Arrow Key** to move the cursor to the beginning of the title.
9. Click the **Right Justification Button** in the **Formatting Toolbar.** The title and page number 1 will shift to the right margin.

MICROSOFT WORD
Line Spacing - Font

TITLE PAGE

APA papers have a specific format for the title page which contains a **running head**, the **title**, the **author's name**, and **affiliation.** **See sample title page on page 9-16.**

1. Move the cursor to the top line of the first page.
2. Type at the left margin the words, **Running Head:,** in upper and lower case followed by a colon, leave one space and type, all in upper case, an **abbreviated title** of fewer than 50 characters including punctuation and spaces.
3. Center the **full title** in upper and lower case on the page. Double space if two or more lines.
4. Center **your name** in upper and lower case one double space below the title.
5. Center **your school name** in upper and lower case one double space below your name.

ABSTRACT PAGE

Formal **APA** papers include an **abstract page** which summarizes the paper. It is always numbered page **2.** **See sample Abstract Page on page 9-17.**

1. Move the cursor to the end of the last word in the **title page.** Press **Enter** to place the cursor on a new blank line.
2. Press **Ctrl + Enter** to begin a new page.
3. Center the word, **Abstract,** in upper and lower case on the top line and double space.
4. Type the abstract, a summary of your paper, in a single paragraph without paragraph indention in fewer than 960 characters including punctuation and spacing.

TEXT

APA papers begin text on the third page. **See sample Text Page on page 9-18.**

1. Move the cursor to the end of the last line of text on the **Abstract Page.** Press **Enter** to place the cursor on a new blank line.
2. Press **Ctrl + Enter** to begin a new page.
3. Center the **title** of your paper in upper and lower case double spaced at the top of the page.
4. Double space and begin typing text.

AUTHOR -DATE CITATIONS

APA papers use a simple system of citing sources by stating the author's name and date of publication of the work in parentheses. Citations are placed directly in the text. No special keystrokes are necessary. The citations lead readers to the alphabetical list of sources in the **References** list at the end of the paper. **Follow the explanation and examples on pages 9-2 and 9-3.**

1. Citations are placed directly in the text. No special keystrokes are necessary.

MICROSOFT WORD
Line Spacing - Font

REFERENCES LIST

The **References** list is printed at the end of the paper and presents full bibliographic information for every source cited in the body of your paper. Do not include sources you may have consulted, but did not use. It is a good idea to prepare the **References** list before you actually start writing the paper so you will know how to cite the references in the text. **See sample formats for References entries on pages 9-4 through 9-11 and the sample References Page on page 9-20.**

1. Move the cursor to the end of the last line of text. Press Enter to place the cursor on a new blank line.
2. Press **Ctrl + Enter** to begin a new page.
3. Center the word, **References,** in upper and lower case on the top line. Double space.
4. Type the entries in alphabetical order using the appropriate format for the type of reference you are citing.
5. Indent the first line of each entry one half inch. Double space within and between entries.

TABLES

Tables should be used sparingly. Use them only when data will be better presented in tabular form. Avoid confusing the reader by breaking up text with too many tables. Do not duplicate information in the text which appears in a table. A table should supplement material in the text, but it should also be understandable alone.

Tables are assigned arabic numerals and brief titles and are located as close as possible to their mention in the text on a separate page. Every column must have a short heading. The data in the left column usually describes the major independent variable.

Use horizontal rules only and use vertical spacing to make the table easily readable. Double space within tables. **See the sample Table on page 9-19.**

Although **Microsoft Word 6** and **7** have programs to set up tables automatically, **APA** tables are very simple with no vertical rules and only a few horizontal rules. The easiest and quickest way to prepare tables is with tabs.

1. Press **Ctrl + Enter** to begin a new page.
2. Type **Table 1** flush left in upper and lower case without a period on the top line.
3. Double space and type the **title** flush left and underlined. Capitalize only the first letters of major words. Extra lines of title are flush left and double spaced.
4. Double space and type a **solid line** across the page by pressing **Shift** and **Underline Keys**.
5. You must now set up the rows and columns which make up the table. Each column must have a header and these should be evenly spaced across the top of the table. Leave at least three spaces between columns.

Setting Tabs for Headers

6. Look at the extreme left end of the ruler. You will see a **Tab Alignment Button** with an **L-shaped marker**. Each time you click on it the marker will change to an **upside down T**, a **backwards L**, or an **upside down T with a dot**. The **L-shape** is the **Tab Alignment Button** for **aligning text at the left letter**, the **upside down T** is for **centering text at the tab**, the **backwards L** is for **aligning text at the**

right letter, and the **upside down T with a dot** is for **aligning numbers at a decimal point.**

7. Click on the **Tab Alignment Button** until it changes to the **upside down T.**

8. Click in the ruler to set a tab at the approximate location where the first header should be. Continue the process by clicking in the ruler at the approximate locations where each header should be.

9. Press the **Tab Key** and type the first header. It will be centered at the tab location. Follow the same procedure with the remaining headers. If the spacing doesn't look right, select a header you would like to move, click on its **Tab** and drag it left or right until the spacing looks correct. The headers will move with the **Tabs** as you move them.

10. Double space and type a **solid line** under the headers.

Entering Data

11. Double space and enter data in each column by pressing the **Tab Key** to move the cursor to the next column. Double space between rows.

12. Adjust spacing by dragging the tab stop to a new location on the ruler. Remove unwanted tab stops by simply dragging them off the ruler.

13. If you are entering decimal data, click on the **Tab Alignment Button** until it changes to an **upside down T with a dot**. Decimal data will be aligned on the decimal points.

14. Double space after entering data and type a **solid line.** Double space to place the cursor on a new line.

Reset Default Tab Settings

15. Choose **Tabs** from the **Format Menu.** The **Tabs Dialog Box** will appear. Click **Clear All.** The tabs you set for the table will disappear.

16. Use the **Up** and **Down Arrows** to set **.5"** in the **Default Tab Stops Box.** Click **OK.** The default tabs will be set.

17. Double space and press **Ctrl + Enter** to start a new page. Continue typing your paper.

**MICROSOFT WORD
Line Spacing - Font**

SPELL CHECK

Word 6 - Word 7 - Word 97 - Word 2000

1. Choose **Spelling** from the **Tools Menu.** The **Spelling Dialog Box** will open.
2. Misspelled words will appear in the **Not in Dictionary Box** with the correctly spelled word in the **Change to** or **Suggestons Box.** Other variations of the word will appear in the **Suggestions Scroll Box.**
3. If the correct word is in the **Change to Box**, click **Change** or **Change All** to correct the word wherever it appears in the paper.
4. If the word you want is in the **Suggestions Scroll List**, click on it and then click **Change.**
5. If the word is correctly spelled as is, and **Word's Spell Check** does not recognize it, click **Ignore.**

Word 7 - Word 97 - Word 2000   Automatic Spell Checking

Word will place a ragged, red underline under misspelled words as you type.

1. Choose **Options** from the **Tools Menu.** Choose the **Spelling and Grammar Tab** and be sure there is a check on the **Automatic Spell Checking** or **Check Spelling as You Type option.** If not, click on it.
2. Click the **right mouse button** on the misspelled word. A list of **replacement words** will appear.
3. Click on the **correct replacement word** or click **Ignore All.** If it is a special word, click on **Add** to add the word to the **dictionary.**

PRINTING

Word 6

1. Choose **Print** from the **File Menu.** The **Print Dialog Box** will appear.
2. If you are using your computer in a lab and there are several printers, click on **Printer** to be sure you are using the correct printer. The **Print Setup Dialog Box** will appear showing the **Default Printer.** If it is the correct printer, click on **Cancel.** If not, click on the correct printer in the **Printers Scroll List** and click on **Set as Default Printer.** The **Print Dialog Box** will reappear.
3. Be sure **Document** is displayed in the **Print What** list. Use the **Up** or **Down Arrows** in the **Copies Box** to select the number of copies you want to print. Click on one of the **Buttons** in the **Page Range Box.** If you want to print selected pages, separate individual pages by commas and series of pages by a hyphen. For example, if you type: 5, 9-12, 15 the printer will print pages 5, 9, 10, 11, 12, and 15.

Word 7 - Word 97 - Word 2000

1. Choose **Print** from the **File Menu.** The **Print Dialog Box** will appear.
2. If you are using your computer in a lab and there are several printers, click on the down arrow at the right end of the **Printer Box.** All available printers will be displayed. Click on the correct printer.
3. Be sure **Document** is displayed in the **Print What list.** Use the **Up** or **Down Arrows** in the **Number of Copies Box** to select the copies you want to print. Click the **Down Arrow** in the **Print Box** if you want to print a range of pages. If you want to print selected pages, separate individual pages by commas and series of pages by a hyphen. For example, if you type: 5, 9-12, 15 the printer will print pages 5, 9, 10, 11, 12, and 15.

> **MICROSOFT WORD**
> **Line Spacing - Font**

SAVING

Word 6

1. Choose **Save** from the **File Menu** or click the **Save Button** in the **Standard Toolbar.** It is the third button from the left and has a picture of a floppy disk on it. The first time you save a document, **Word** will open the **Save As Dialog Box.**
2. The **Insertion Point** will be blinking in the **File Name Box.** Type the name of your document. It may have no more than 8 characters and no commas, periods, or spaces. **Word** will assign an **extension** of three characters called **doc.**
3. Check that **drive C** is selected in the **Drives: Box.** This is the usual designation for the hard drive.
4. Choose a **Directory** where you want to save your document in the **Directories: Scroll List. Winword** is as good a directory as any.
5. Click on **OK.**
6. To avoid disaster, click on the **Save Button** in the **Standard Toolbar** every ten or fifteen minutes. **Word** will save your work instantly to the hard drive and directory you selected in the **Save As Dialog Box.**
7. An easy way to save your work is to turn on **Automatic Save.** Click on the **Options Button** in the **Save As Dialog Box.** Enter the interval in minutes in the **Automatic Save Every Box.** Ten minutes is good for most people. Type **10.**
8. It is a good idea to save your document on another disk just in case the hard drive crashes or some other glitch which computers are known for develops. Choose **Save As** from the **File Menu.** The **Save As Dialog Box** will appear.

9. Insert a **floppy disk** in the **A: Drive.** Use the **down arrow** in the **Drives Scroll List** until the **A: Drive** appears.

10. Click **OK.** Your document will be saved on the floppy disk. Remove it and keep it in a safe place. Repeat the process when you finish working each day.

Word 7 - Word 97 - Word 2000

1. Choose **Save** from the **File Menu** or click the **Save Button** in the **Standard Toolbar.** It is the third button from the left and has a picture of a floppy disk on it. The first time you save a document, **Word** will open the **Save As Dialog Box.**

2. Select the folder in which you want to save your document in the **Save in: Box.**

3. Type the name of your document in the **File Name Box.** **Word 7, Word 97, and Word 2000** allows you to use up to **255** characters. **Word** will assign an **extension** of three characters called **doc.**

4. Click on **Save.**

5. To avoid disaster, click on the **Save Button** in the **Standard Toolbar** every ten or fifteen minutes. **Word** will save your work instantly to the folder you selected in the **Save As Dialog Box.**

6. An easy way to save your work is to turn on **Automatic Save.** Click on Tools and General **Options** in the **Save As Dialog Box.** Enter the interval in minutes in the **Automatic Save Every Box or the Auto Recover Info Every: in Windows 2000.** Ten minutes is good for most people. Type **10.**

7. It is a good idea to save your document on another disk just in case the hard drive crashes or some other glitch which computers are known for develops. Choose **Save As** from the **File Menu.** The **Save As Dialog Box** will appear.

8. Insert a **floppy disk** in the **floppy drive.** Select **A:** in the **Save in: drop down list.**

9. Click **OK.** Your document will be saved on the floppy disk. Remove it and keep it in a safe place. Repeat the process when you finish working each day.

American Psychological Association
Author-Date Citation
With Microsoft Works

OPENING MICROSOFT WORKS FIRST TIME

Windows 3. 1 - Works 3. 0
1. At the **DOS** prompt, **C:\>** type win and press **Enter.** The **Program Manager Window** will appear with several icons.
2. Double click on the the **Microsoft Works group icon.** The **Works group window** will open.
3. Double click on the **Microsoft Works icon**. The **Startup Dialog Box** will appear.
4. Click on **Word Processor.** A blank **Microsoft Works Document Window** will appear similar to the one shown below with a **Menu Bar and Toolbar**. The cursor or insertion point will be flashing at the left margin. You are ready to being typing your paper.

Windows 95 - Works 4. 0
1. Click on the **Start Button** in the lower left corner of your screen.
2. Drag the pointer up to **Programs.** The **Programs Menu** will pop up.
3. Drag the pointer to **Microsoft Works 4.0.** Another **Menu** will pop up. Drag the pointer to **Microsoft Works 4.0.** The **Works Task Launcher** will open.
4. Click on the **Works Tools Tab** at the upper right corner. Click on **Word Processor.** A blank **Works Document Window** will open similar to the one shown below with a **Menu Bar**, **Toolbar**, **Title Bar** and **Ruler.** The cursor or insertion point will be flashing at the left margin. You are ready to begin typing your paper.

MICROSOFT WORKS 4.0 DOCUMENT PAGE WINDOW

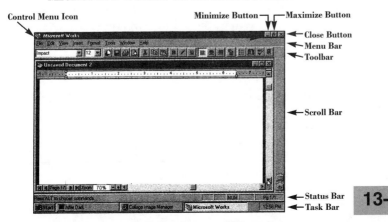

Control Menu Icon — Minimize Button — Maximize Button — Close Button — Menu Bar — Toolbar — Scroll Bar — Status Bar — Task Bar

OPENING YOUR DOCUMENT LATER

Windows 3. 1 Works 3. 0

1. Follow the steps above to open **Microsoft Works.**
2. Choose **Open Existing File** from the **Startup Dialog Box.**
3. Click on the file which you have named for your paper in the **File Name List** in the **Open Dialog Box.** Click **OK.** The **Document Window** will open with your paper.

Windows 95 Works 4. 0

1. Follow the steps above to open **Microsoft Works.**
2. Choose **Open** from the **File Menu**.
3. Click on the file which you have named for your paper in the **File List.** If it is not there, use the **Down Arrow** to scroll through the **Look In Box** to locate the folder in which you saved your document.

MARGINS

The setting for **APA** papers is one inch on top, bottom, and sides. You can change the margins if required by your instructor, but do not right justify or hyphenate words.

1. Choose **Page Setup** from the **File Menu.** The **Page Setup Dialog Box** will appear.
2. Choose the **Margins Tab** and enter **1"** in the **Top, Bottom, Left Margin,** and **Right Margin Boxes**.
3. Click **OK.**

LINE SPACING

APA papers are double spaced throughout. The default setting for **Microsoft Works** is single spacing. Change the setting before you begin typing.

Works 3. 0

1. Choose **Paragraph** from the **Format Menu.** The **Paragraph Dialog Box** will appear.
2. Click on the **Breaks** and **Spacing Tab.**
3. Enter **2** in the **Between Lines Box** and click **OK.**

MICROSOFT WORKS
Margins - Line Spacing

Works 4. 0

1. Choose **Paragraph** from the **Format Menu.** The **Paragraph Dialog Box** will appear.
2. Click on the **Spacing Tab** and use the **Up Arrow** in the **Line Spacing Box** to change the setting to **2 li.**
3. Click **OK.**

FONT

Font is the term used to describe the shape of the type used in typing. The **APA** suggests using a standard typeface in 10 or 12 point size similar to that found in typewriters. **Courier** and **Times Roman** are good examples. Although **Microsoft Works** enables you to change the font, the size, and a whole range of styles such as bold, condensed, and shadow, select one simple typeface and keep it in the plain text style.

```
    This is 12 point Courier font.
```

1. Click on the **Font Pop-up Menu** in the **Tool Bar.** Drag down to **Courier** or **Times New Roman.**
2. Click on the **Type Size Pop-up Menu** in the **Tool Bar.** Drag down to **12.**

or

1. Choose **Font and Style** from the **Format Menu.** The **Format Font** and **Style Dialog Box** will open.
2. Use the scroll arrows to select **Courier** or **Times New Roman** and click **OK.**

ITALICS AND UNDERLINING

Underlining is used to indicate words which are to be italicized in a printed version. Writers following **APA** style should not use italics unless approved by the instructor. The titles of books, periodicals, volume numbers in reference lists, some test scores, and Latin scientific terms are underlined to indicate italics.

1. Select the text you want to underline or italicize.
2. Click on the *I* or U buttons in the **Tool Bar.**

CENTERING AND JUSTIFYING

Justification describes how words are placed on the page: flush left, flush right, or centered. **Microsoft Works** allows you to spread the words on each line across the page so the right margin is straight or right justified. Although **APA** papers should not be justified, you will need to center or move some text at times.

1. Select the text you want to center or move.
2. Click on the **Left, Right** or **Center Justification Buttons** in the **Toolbar.** The are just to the right of the **B,** *I,* **U, Buttons.**

or

3. Press **Ctrl+L** to align left, **Ctrl+E** to center, **Ctrl+R** to align right, or **Ctrl+J** to justify.

INDENTION

APA papers are indented one half inch. The **Microsoft Works** default setting is one half inch, but you may want to change indents for quotations or other purposes.

1. Choose **Paragraph** from the **Format Menu.** The **Paragraph Dialog Box** will appear.
2. Click on the **Indents** and **Alignment Tab.**
3. Enter .5" in the **First Line Indent Box.**
4. Enter any other changes you need in the **Left, Right,** and **First Line** boxes.
5. Click on **OK.**

PAGINATION

Beginning with the first page, **APA** papers carry a right justified heading one half inch from the top of the page with the first two or three words of the title of your paper in upper and lower case followed by the page number in arabic numerals. **See sample pages on pages 9-16 through 9-20.**

1. Choose **Headers** and **Footers** from the **View Menu.** The **Headers** and **Footers Dialog Box** will open.
2. Type an **ampersand** and **small r** like this (**&r**) followed by the first two or three words of the title of your paper. Press the **space bar** five times to move the cursor five spaces to the right and type an **ampersand** and a **small p** like this (**&p**).
3. Click OK. The header will contain the first two or three words of your title and the page number at the right margin.
4. Choose **Print Preview** in the **File Menu** to see how the header looks on the page.

TITLE PAGE

APA papers have a specific format for the title page which contains a **running head**, the **title**, the **author's name**, and **affiliation. See sample title page on page 9-16.**

1. Move the cursor to the top line of the first page.
2. Type at the left margin the words, **Running Head:** in upper and lower case followed by a colon, leave one space and type, all in upper case, an **abbreviated title** of fewer than 50 characters including punctuation and spaces.
3. Center the **full title** in upper and lower case on the page. Double space if two or more lines.
4. Center **your name** in upper and lower case one double space below the title.
5. Center **your school name** in upper and lower case one double space below your name.

ABSTRACT PAGE

Formal **APA** papers include an **abstract page** which summarizes the paper. It is always numbered page 2. **See sample Abstract Page on page 9-17.**

1. Move the cursor to the end of the last word of the **title page**. Press **Enter** to place the cursor on a new blank line.
2. Choose **Page Break** from the **Insert Menu.** A dotted line will appear across the page with a new page symbol. The status bar at the bottom of the screen will indicate the next page number.

3. Center the word, **Abstract**, in upper and lower case on the top line and double space.
4. Type the abstract, a summary of your paper, in a single paragraph without paragraph indention in fewer than 960 characters including punctuation and spacing.

TEXT

APA papers begin on the third page. **See the sample Text Page on page 9-18.**

1. Move the cursor to the end of the last line of text on the **Abstract Page**. Press **Enter** to place the cursor on a new blank line.
2. Choose **Page Break** from the **Insert Menu**. A dotted line will appear across the page with a new page symbol. The status bar at the bottom of the screen will indicate the next page number.
3. Center the **title** of your paper in upper and lower case double spaced at the top of the page.
4. Double space and begin typing text.

AUTHOR-DATE CITATIONS

APA papers use a simple system of citing sources by stating the author's name and date of publication of the work in parentheses. Citations are placed directly in the text. No special keystrokes are necessary. The citations lead readers to the alphabetical list of sources in the **References** list at the end of the paper. **Follow the explanation and examples of parenthetical citations on pages 9-2 and 9-3.**

1. Citations are placed directly in the text. No special keystrokes are necessary.

REFERENCES LIST

The **References** list is printed at the end of the paper and presents the full bibliographic information for every source cited in the body of your paper. Do not include sources you may have consulted, but did not use. It is a good idea to prepare the **References** list before you actually start the paper so you will know how to cite the references in the text. **See the sample formats for References entries on pages 9-4 through 9-11 and the sample References page on page 9-20.**

1. Move the cursor to the end of the last line of text. Press **Enter** to place the cursor on a new blank line.
2. Choose **Page Break** from the **Insert Menu**. A dotted line will appear across the page with a new page symbol. The status bar at the bottom of the screen will indicate the next page number.
3. Center the word, **References**, in upper and lower case on the top line. Double space.
4. Type entries in alphabetical order using the appropriate format for the type of reference you are citing.
5. Indent the first line of each entry one half inch. Double space within and between entries.

TABLES

Tables should be used sparingly. Use them only when data will be better presented in tabular form. Avoid confusing the reader by breaking up text with too many tables. Do not duplicate information in the text which appears in a table. A table should supplement material in the text, but it should also be understandable alone.

Tables are assigned arabic numerals and brief titles and are located as close as possible to their mention in the text on a separate page. Every column must have a short heading. The data in the left column usually describes the major independent variable.

Use horizontal rules only and use horizontal spacing to make the table easily readable. Double space within tables.

MICROSFT WORKS
References - Tables

See the sample Table on page 9-19.

Although **Microsoft Works** has a program to set up tables automatically, **APA** tables are very simple with no vertical rules and only a few horizontal rules. The easiest and quickest way to prepare tables is with tabs.

1. Begin each table on a separate page. Move the cursor to the end of the last line of text. Press **Enter** to place the cursor on a new blank line.

2. Choose **Page Break** from the **Insert Menu**. A dotted line will appear across the page with a new page symbol. The status bar at the bottom of the screen will indicate the next page number.

3. Type **Table 1** flush left in upper and lower case without a period on the top line.

4. Double space and type the **title** flush left and underlined. Capitalize only the first letters of major words. Extra lines of title are flush left and double spaced.

5. Double space and type a solid line across the page by pressing **Shift** and **Underline Keys**.

6. You must now set up the rows and colums which make up the table. Each column must have a header and these should be spaced evenly across the top of the table. Leave at least three spaces between the columns.

Setting Tabs for Headers

7. Double click the **Arrow Pointer** on any **Tab** in the **Ruler**. The **Tabs Dialog Box** will open. Click on **Center** in the **Alignment Box**. Since no leaders are necessary, click on the **None Button** under **Leader**.

8. Look at the ruler and decide where you think the first header should be. For example, you might think it would look right at the one inch mark. Click the **Arrow Pointer** in the **Ruler** at the one inch mark. A **Center Tab Stop** will be placed at that position.

9. Continue the process for each of the headers you need.

10. Press the **Tab Key** and type the next header. It will be centered at the tab location. Follow the same procedure with the remaining headers.

11. Check the spacing to see if the headers are properly spaced. Make adjustments by selecting the header you want to move and dragging its **Tab Stop** to a new location on the ruler. The header will be dragged along with the **Tab Stop**. A bit of trial and error will give you the best spacing in a couple of minutes.

12. Double space and type a solid line under the headers by pressing **Shift** and **Underline Keys**.

MICROSOFT WORKS
Tables

Entering Data

13. Double space and enter numerical data in each column by pressing the **Tab Key** to move the cursor to the next column. Double space between each line of data. If any numerical data contains decimal points, reopen the **Tabs Dialog Box** and click the **Decimal Alignment Button**. Decimal data will be lined up on the decimal points.

14. After entering data, double space and type a solid line across the page by pressing **Shift** and **Underline Keys**.

Resetting Default Tab Settings

15. Double space to place the cursor on a new line. Choose **Tabs** from the **Format Menu**.

16. Click on **Delete All** and **OK**. The **Default Tab** settings of .5 inches will be set.

17. Choose **Page Break** from the **Insert Menu** to start a new page and continue typing your document.

SPELL CHECK

1. Move the cursor to the top line of the first page of your paper.

2. Choose **Spelling** from the **Tools Menu** or click on the **Spelling Button** in the **Toolbar**. It's on the right end of the **Toolbar** and has the letters ABC with a check mark. The **Spelling Dialog Box** will open.

3. **Works** will display the first word which is not in its dictionary next to **Not in Dictionary:** and highlight the word in the **Change To: Box** and in your document.

4. Click on the **Suggest Button** and **Works** will list some suggested changes in the **Suggestions List Box**.

5. Click on the correct spelling in the **Suggestions List Box** and it will appear in the **Change To: Box**.

6. Click on the **Change Button** and the correct word will replace the incorrect spelling in the document. If you wish to change the word every time it appears, click on the **Change All Button**.

7. If the word is unusual or special and is correctly spelled even though it is not in the **Works** dictionary, click the **Ignore** or **Ignore All Button**. If you want to add the special word to the dictionary, click the **Add Button**. To save time, you can click the **Always Suggest Box** to save the step of clicking the **Suggest Button** each time.

PRINTING

1. Choose **Print Preview** from the **File Menu** or click on the **Print Preview Button** on the **Toolbar.** It is the fourth button to the right of the **Font Size Scroll Button.** It has a picture of a folded sheet of paper with a magnifying glass. The document will appear exactly as it will when printed. If you see any errors in spacing or layout, you can make adjustments by returning to the page in the regular view.

2. Choose **Printer Setup** from the **File Menu.** The **Printer Setup Dialog Box** will appear.

3. Use the **Scroll Bars** to view the available printers and click on the one you want to use. Click on **Setup** to change any values necessary. Click on **OK.**

4. Choose **Print** from the **File Menu.** The **Print Dialog Box** will open.

5. Make necessary changes in the **Number of Copies** and **Print Range Boxes.** Click on **OK.**

SAVING

1. Choose **Save As** from the **File Menu.** The **Save As Dialog Box** will open.

2. Type a file name for your document using no more than 8 characters without spaces in the **File Name Box.** The document will be saved to the hard drive, usually C:. Click on **OK.**

3. After you have named your document, choose **Save** from the **File Menu** or press **Ctrl + S** on the **Keyboard** every few minutes to avoid disaster.

4. It is a good idea to save your document to a floppy disk at the end of each session. Insert a formatted floppy in the A: drive.

5. Choose **Save As** from the **File Menu.**

6. Scroll down to the **A: drive** with the **Drives: Scroll Button.** Click on **OK.**